Nien Cheng

Courage in China

Nien Cheng

Courage in China

By Leila Merrell Foster

Consultant: Parris H. Chang, Ph.D.
Professor of Political Science
Director, Center for East Asian Studies
The Pennsylvania State University
University Park, Pennsylvania

ℂℙ CHILDRENS PRESS®

CHICAGO

CIP—Library of Congress Cataloging-in-Publication Data

Foster, Leila Merrell.
    Nien Cheng : courage in China / by Leila Merrell Foster.
        p.   cm.—(People of distinction)
    Includes bibliographical references and index.
    Summary: Traces the life of the brave Chinese woman who
described her years of imprisonment during the Cultural Revolution
in her book, "Life and Death in Shanghai."
    ISBN 0-516-03279-8
    1. Cheng, Nien, 1915-   —Juvenile literature. 2. China—History—
Cultural Revolution, 1966-1969—Juvenile literature. 3. China—
Biography—Juvenile literature. [1. Cheng, Nien, 1915-   .2. China—
History—Cultural Revolution, 1966-1969. 3. China—Biography.]
I. Title. II. Series : People of distinction biographies.
CT1828.C5248F67   1992
951.05′6′092—dc20
[B]   92-9333
                                                                                CIP
                                                                                 AC

1 2 3 4 5 6 7 8 9 10 R 99 98 97 96 95 94 93 92

ACKNOWLEDGMENTS
The editors would like to acknowledge use of excerpted material from the following works:

Life and Death in Shanghai by Nien Cheng, published by Grove Press, Inc. and Grafton Books, an imprint of HarperCollins Publishers Limited. Copyright © Nien Cheng, 1986.

Christianity Today, "The Resolve to Resist" by E. Vaughn. May 13, 1988.

National Review, "Massacre in Peking" by Nien Cheng. August 4, 1989.

New Choices for the Best Years, "A Voice of Hope for China" by C. Reeve. September 1989.

PICTURE ACKNOWLEDGMENTS
AP/Wide World Photos—32, 48 (2 photos), 49 (2 photos), 52 (2 photos), 53 (bottom), 54, 78: © Tom Victor, 2

© Mary Noble Ours—4, 8, 10, 50 (bottom), 51 (bottom), 96

Photo Courtesy of Slippery Rock University, Slippery Rock, Pennsylvania—50 (top)

Gamma-Liaison—© Piero Guerrini, 51 (top), 53 (top)

Cover illustration by Len W. Meents

Project Editor: Mary Reidy
Designer: Karen Yops

Table of Contents

Chapter 1

REVOLUTIONARY ACTION

"Bam, bam, bam!" The pounding on the front gate started and at the same time the doorbell rang without stopping. Inside the home of Nien Cheng in Shanghai, China, her servant announced in an unsteady voice: "They have come!"[1]

Telling him to keep calm and to open the gate without saying anything, Nien Cheng awaited the onslaught of the young people who called themselves the Red Guards.

The Red Guards were radical teenagers and young adult students organized in 1966 by Chairman Mao Zedong, the leader of the Communist party and founder of the People's Republic of China. As more students joined the Red Guards, the government decided to close all schools indefinitely. The Red Guards traveled around the country zealously carrying out the "Cultural Revolution." They intended to change beliefs and teach Mao's ideas, which had been published in four volumes entitled *The Collected Works of Mao Zedong* and in *The Little Red Book*, a collection of Mao's writing and speeches. Many of the Red Guards' victims were teachers, party officials, and others in high places.

During the late summer of 1966 the Red Guards and party leaders became increasingly violent. They printed posters denouncing others and took part in break-ins, public humiliations, beatings, and fighting. About 40 percent of all the students in China belonged to different Red Guard units. Students of *bourgeois* origin (middle class with capitalist views) were admitted to units if they renounced and denounced their origins.

It had been a peaceful summer night, that August 30, 1966. However, Nien Cheng had been expecting such an invasion of her home. She knew her time must surely come because of her connections in the past with Shell International Petroleum Company, a foreign oil company with offices in Shanghai. She picked up the keys to her house and a copy of the Constitution of the People's Republic of China.

"Open the gate! Open the gate! Are you all dead? Why don't you open the gate?"[2] The Red Guards continued to pound on the gate. The horn from their truck added to the noise. These groups of young people had been organized by a faction within the Communist leadership of China to raid the homes of the wealthy.

As Nien Cheng descended the stairs to the first floor, she tried to appear calm and resigned to what she knew would happen. As she reached the bottom step, the Red Guards burst into her home and announced: "We are the Red Guards. We have come to take revolutionary action against you!"[3]

The thirty or forty high school students between the ages of fifteen and twenty were led by three older persons — probably their teachers. All wore the arm band of the Red Guard. Their "revolutionary action" consisted of looting homes and gathering up what they considered useful for distribution by the government. They also stole objects and vandalized property.

Nien Cheng held up the constitution she had carried downstairs. In a calm voice she stated: "It's against the Constitution of the People's Republic of China to enter a private house without a search warrant."[4] One of the young men seized the document and threw it on the floor, stating that the constitution had been abolished and that in its place were the teachings of the great leader Chairman Mao.

One of the young girls shook her fist under the nose of Nien Cheng and spat on the floor. "What trick are you trying to play? Your only way out is to bow your head in submission. Otherwise you will suffer."[5] Another of the young Guards smashed a mirror, tore the frame off the wall, and threw it against the stairs. Then the Guards all read aloud from a book of quotations from Mao Zedong: "When the enemies with guns are annihilated, the enemies without guns still remain. We must not belittle these enemies."[6]

They ordered Nien Cheng to hand over her keys. She placed them on a chest in the hall. The Guards spread out to different rooms, and Nien Cheng was taken to the dining room and locked in.

Nien Cheng was a widow. Her only daughter was away from home that evening at the film studio where she worked. When Nien Cheng's husband had died of cancer in 1957, he had been general manager of the Shanghai office of Shell. After his death, Nien Cheng had worked for Shell with the title of "adviser to management" until the spring of 1966, when the company closed its office.

Because of her work and her foreign friends, Nien Cheng had been able to maintain a high standard of living in a house filled with beautiful Chinese antiques and Western luxuries. She had been careful not to flaunt these riches in a Communist society.

Nien Cheng had three or four servants. When the Communists had gained control in Shanghai, they had required rich families to continue employing their servants. Nien Cheng's servants were very loyal to her, and she had tried to protect them during this invasion by the Red Guards by telling them to go to their rooms and stay out of harm's way.

This night was the beginning of what was to become almost seven years of imprisonment and harassment for Nien Cheng. She would write a book about her experiences entitled *Life and Death in Shanghai*.

Never had the dining room in which she had been placed looked so beautiful. The black wood dining room table surface shone with polish. The antique plates, vases, and figures that Nien Cheng had collected over the years were displayed to perfection. She knew that the paintings she loved so much might well be destroyed because some of the artists were no longer in favor with the Communist party.

As she listened to the loud noises overhead from the second floor, Mrs. Cheng said good-bye to these treasures that had meant so much to her. When Nien Cheng heard someone approach the dining room, she called out asking for the door to be opened. She needed to go to the bathroom. One of the Guards took her upstairs. She was amazed to see one of the young Guards crushing a delicate porcelain wine cup with his foot.

On impulse, Nien Cheng leaped forward and caught the young Guard just as he had lifted his foot to crush another cup. They tumbled on the floor. While Nien Cheng was looking around to see that they had not fallen on the treasure, the Guard kicked her in the chest. She cried out in pain. The other Guards came rushing over to see what was going on. They accused her of trying to protect her possessions. Nien Cheng denied this and quoted back to them the teachings of Mao, that she should be allowed to give her reasons. She pointed to the modern loot of cameras, binoculars, and watches that the Guards had set aside to be given to the government. Those items, she said, could be replaced, but the wine cup was three hundred years old and part of their cultural heritage. It could not be reproduced.

The Guards rejected her argument saying, "The purpose of the Great Proletarian Revolution is to destroy the old culture. You cannot stop us!"[7]

Nien Cheng knew she would have to try another tactic. She

reminded the Guards that she had surrendered her keys to them without a struggle. She pointed out that the treasures she was trying to save had been made by workers centuries ago. Their labor should be respected. She urged them to take the antiques to the Shanghai Museum admitting that she should not have kept them to herself because they belonged to all the people.

One of the girls replied that the museum was closed and that the experts there were under investigation. Not only the capitalists associated with private companies but also the intellectuals were to be destroyed.

Nien Cheng then suggested that they take the treasures to one of the officials in Shanghai whom they trusted, because there must be some policy covering private collections. The Guards called her a "class enemy" and replied that the only policy was in the book of quotations of Mao.

Nien Cheng said she had seen a placard that said "Long Live World Revolution." She asked if they didn't realize that they could finance their world revolution with the money that could be collected in Hong Kong for these items. The antiques were extremely valuable.

Now she had their interest. It made the Guards feel important to think that they could help finance the propagation of communism. Mrs. Cheng asked them to put the antiques back into their boxes and take them to be sold or given to a museum as they thought right, according to the teachings of Mao.

One of the teachers asked how much her treasures were really worth. When Nien Cheng replied at least a million yuan, the teacher called the Guards into a conference. Nien Cheng started putting the antiques back into their boxes and returning them to the cupboard in which they were kept. At the cupboard, she saw many of the treasures had already been broken. The floor was covered with porcelain chips from the antiques.

The third-floor rooms were a mess. Fur coats and evening dresses had been cut with scissors. Food staples that had been stored there lay open and spilled on top of clothing. Furniture had been pulled out of place and overturned.

Tired and with her chest throbbing with pain, Nien Cheng sought some place to lie down. She went into her daughter's bedroom, the one room still undisturbed. Through the window, she saw a bonfire on the lawn. The Guards were tossing her books into the fire.

Soon Mrs. Cheng was interrupted by a Guard who told her that she was needed in another room. She was taken to her study where a thin girl sat tensely at the desk. As Nien Cheng was seated by the desk, the girl gave her a frightened look.

The teacher in the room asked Nien Cheng to account for the jewelry that was in a box and on the desk. "Is this all the jewelry you have? Look it over and tell us if everything is here.... Speak the truth. We are going to check with your servants."[8]

Everyone else in the room stopped to hear Nien Cheng's answer. It was clear that the girl at the desk was suspected of having stolen some of the items. Such a practice was not at all unusual, and the temptation for the poorer Guards must have been great.

Trying to minimize the problem for the girl, Nien Cheng replied that the most important items were there, but that a watch, some rings, and a gold bracelet were missing. The girl at the desk was almost in tears. Nien Cheng was asked to describe the items. While doing so, she also suggested that they look on the floor to see if perhaps they had dropped in the tissue paper that littered the floor.

Immediately the girl ducked under the desk along with some of the other Guards and came up smiling because the rings and the bracelet had been found. The watch was not found, but probably it had been taken by someone else. The teacher looked quizzically at Nien Cheng because she guessed that Mrs. Cheng had given the girl the chance to "find" the missing items and save herself.

At last, Nien Cheng was permitted to sleep and in the morning to eat breakfast. A liaison officer from the Shanghai municipal government arrived to ask how she had been treated. (Soon even this check on the conduct of the Red Guards was to be abandoned.) Nien Cheng responded that she had been allowed to eat and sleep and that the Red Guards had carried out their revolutionary action in accord with the teachings of

Chairman Mao. The guards standing around were pleased with her reply.

The official then informed her that she would no longer have the use of her entire house—only a room and enough furniture to live like an average worker. Nien Cheng did not respond. The official further advised Nien Cheng that she should pack a suitcase with warm clothing because she would not have any central heating in the house. Coal was needed for industry.

One of the Guards delegated to supervise the packing of Mrs. Cheng's suitcase had gone home after his night's work at her house and then returned in the morning. He was upset because he discovered that while he had been engaged in a revolutionary action at her house, some other Red Guards had looted his home. It seems that though both his father and grandfather had been workers, an aunt living with them had once owned a fruit stall in Shanghai and so was also to be considered a capitalist. The boy, shocked by his own experience, was willing to help Nien Cheng pack a suitcase of clothes for her daughter along with a canvas bag of bedding.

By late afternoon, the Red Guards had left. Nien Cheng cautioned her servants not to clean up the mess that had been left behind for fear that they would be accused of stealing. The servants just cleared a path around the mess.

Soon, the doorbell rang again. The servant reported that another group of Red Guards had arrived. This time there were eight middle-aged men with the red arm band of the

Guards. This new group, hardly the right age to be Red Guards, was disappointed that the best loot had been taken. They packed a few suitcases and left.

Nien Cheng's daughter, Meiping, returned. On the outside gate was a poster that translated to "inside communicate foreign countries." It was the equivalent of calling Nien Cheng a foreign spy. When Meiping saw her mother standing in the middle of the mess, she ran to her and put her arms around her. Nien Cheng told her not to be upset. Someday, when the Cultural Revolution was over, they would rebuild. Her daughter doubted that anyone would again be allowed to have a house as beautiful as theirs had been.

Nien Cheng cautioned her daughter not to look back, but to look ahead. Possessions were not important. As long as they still had each other they could be happy. Her daughter promised that the two of them would meet the future together. Meiping said: "Don't lose heart!...I love China! I love my country even though it is not always good or right."[9] Tears came to the eyes of Nien Cheng. Though now an outcast, she, too, loved the land of her ancestors.

Chapter 2

BEFORE THE CULTURAL REVOLUTION

Nien was born in 1915, in Beijing, into the distinguished Yao family. She was named after her father's mother. Her father was vice-minister of the navy. Her mother and father's marriage had been arranged by their families, as was customary early in the twentieth century.

Nien's family was very traditional, yet her grandfather showed concern in training his sons for a modern China. When the Red Guards ransacked Nien Cheng's Shanghai home in 1966, they came across old letters from her grandfather to her father when her father was a student in the Japanese naval college. The letters dated from before the 1911 Revolution that changed China from a monarchy to a republic.

One of the adult liaison officers to the Guards commented: "Your grandfather was a patriot even though he was a big landlord. He sent your father, his eldest son, to Japan to learn to become a naval officer because China suffered defeat in the naval battle against Japan in 1895. He also took part in the abortive Constitutional Reform Movement. When that failed, he returned to his native province and devoted himself to academic work."[1]

This view of her family during the Cultural Revolution was

not typical. Nien Cheng was accused of being a descendant of a big landlord family that owned ten thousand mou (roughly seventeen hundred acres) of good agricultural land. Her grandfather was called "a dirty landlord and an advocate of feudalism," because he had written history books in which he had praised several of the emperors. He had been a founder and shareholder in the Hanyehping Steel Complex.

Nien was the eldest child in a family of seven children, three other girls and three boys. Nien and four of her siblings were sent abroad for some of their studies. Two sisters went to the United States, married there, and became American citizens. Because of war and conditions in China, the youngest brother and sister were not able to go to foreign countries for studies.

As was customary in wealthy families, Nien was sent to a girl's boarding school, the Nankai School. There she excelled, becoming president of the student union, working on the school newspaper, and winning oratorical contests. She was good at sports, too. Basketball and track and field were her favorites. History was the subject that she liked best, and there were no courses she really hated. She went on to study at Beijing University. When she was twenty years old she enrolled at the London School of Economics in England, where she majored in economics.

Nien's education was different from the education American children receive. She had to memorize a great deal. One advantage of her training was that she has acquired a superb memory—much better than her American friends. The disadvantage of her education was that it did not encourage people to be creative. She thinks that a blend of the two forms of education would be better.

The two most important ideals instilled in Nien by her family were loyalty and discipline. She was expected to be loyal to her family, her country, and her friends. Self-discipline was valued highly also. Nien was expected to be able to control her impulses. She studied very hard because she could not disappoint her family by getting poor grades. Nien exemplified these ideals of loyalty and discipline in the ordeal that she was to face as an adult.

In 1935, Nien went abroad to continue her studies. She had been sent to Great Britain rather than the United States because a family friend was the Chinese ambassador in London and could keep an eye on her. It was at the London School of Economics that Nien met her husband.

Kang-chi Cheng was a graduate student at the London School of Economics, from which he received his Ph.D. degree. He was a reserved, scholarly young man, who was five years older than Nien. He was a Christian, and Nien was not. Both his mother and his father were Christians and had been educated in Christian schools.

Nien came from a traditional family. They believed in ancestor worship. Her father had no interest in religion, and her mother was a Buddhist. When Nien and Kang-chi became engaged, Kang-chi Cheng wrote his mother that they must try to convert her.

Nien and Kang-chi were married in a London church. Nien went to church with Kang-chi and began to read the Bible. Later, in 1950, when her mother-in-law came to live with the couple, Nien read the Bible to her mother-in-law, whose eyesight was failing. During the seven years before her death, Nien's mother-in-law was an important influence in Nien's growth as a Christian.

In 1940 after World War II had begun, Nien Cheng took a British passenger steamer from England that stopped in New York and then went on to China. Some of the passengers were interviewed in a radio program in New York. Nien Cheng praised the British war effort. She talked of the courage the British were showing during this period of bombing by the Germans.

In China, Kang-chi Cheng became a diplomatic officer for the ruling Kuomintang (Nationalists or National People's party) government. Life could not have been easy in China during this period of war with Japan. The Chengs were in Chongqing (formerly Chungking) during the years 1939 to 1941 when the Japanese bombed the city. Nien Cheng went to a bomb shelter under her house. Her husband had a bomb shelter at his office. In Chongqing, the shelters were often in deep caves in the mountainsides.

In the summer of 1941, a Japanese bomb landed on the

tennis court in front of the Cheng's house; it tore off the roof and caved in part of the house. Nien Cheng lost almost all her possessions at that time. She and her husband were just getting ready to leave with other diplomats to establish a diplomatic base in Canberra, Australia. Nien had placed some of their packed suitcases under a stairway when the air raid began. Although the stairs collapsed, she was able to dig out three suitcases that were badly damaged. She did not have time to dig out the furniture, and she had to buy almost everything new when they reached Hong Kong.

Until the 1966 raid by the Red Guards, Nien had never told her daughter the story of having to start over because of the bombing. However, Nien Cheng carried memories with her of corpses that were dug out of the rubble of Chongqing.

Australia, where they were posted in the diplomatic service, carried happier memories for Nien. On August 18, 1942, her daughter was born. In Sydney, Australia, she watched Meiping as a toddler play in the sand at the beach. With her was a Chinese friend and her little girl, Hean, for whom Nien Cheng was godmother. Both families were soon to return to China.

Kang-chi Cheng was director of the Shanghai office of the ministry of foreign affairs for the Kuomintang government in China in 1949. This was the year that the Communists took over the government, forcing the Kuomintang officials to flee to Taiwan, where, in exile, they claimed to be the legitimate government for all of China. They called themselves the Republic of China.

Chinese officials had to choose whether they would go with the Kuomintang government to Taiwan or remain in China. Early in 1949, Nien Cheng and Meiping were in Hong Kong, a city under British control. Her husband asked her to return to Shanghai and then told her that he had decided to remain in China. Nien Cheng and her husband were idealistic. They hoped that the Communists would unite the country and improve the standard of living for the Chinese people. They, with many other intellectuals of that time, did not foresee the class struggle that the Communists would impose on the educated population.

Kang-chi Cheng was asked by the Communist vice-minister of foreign affairs to join the foreign ministry of the people's government. He declined. Many of the intellectuals who joined the Communist government were later put in prison because of suspicions of their loyalty. Instead, in 1950, Kang-chi became the general manager of the Shanghai branch of Shell International Petroleum Company with the permission of the Communist government.

In 1950 Nien Cheng suffered from tuberculosis of the kidney, and one of her kidneys was removed. This condition meant that she had to be careful of her health and drink a great deal of water to help her remaining kidney function.

The Chengs now led a glamorous life in some ways. They

were expected to entertain and to socialize with the foreign diplomats and business executives. They were able to enjoy the best of the Chinese and the Western worlds. As manager, Kang-chi Cheng talked with high-level Chinese officials on behalf of the Shell company without having to use an interpreter. Passports for the Chengs were approved by no less an official than Prime Minister Zhou Enlai because China wanted to purchase things and get expert help from Shell. The Chengs made several trips to Hong Kong and Europe and the home offices of Shell.

In 1957 Kang-chi Cheng died of cancer. He was only forty-seven years old and had known about his condition for only a year. His death was a shock to Nien Cheng, who was widowed at forty-two years of age. She had depended heavily on her husband. Now she had to train herself to make her own decisions. Her faith in God was a great help to her in getting through this period.

Shell sent in a British employee to take over the position of general manager, but asked Nien Cheng to be a special adviser. She assisted with negotiations between the company and the government and between the company and the labor union. She also managed the staff and served as acting general manager when the British manager was away. She held this position until 1966, when Shell pulled out of China. Shell entered into an agreement turning over its assets and its employment and pension obligations to a Chinese government agency.

Nien Cheng, as part of the management team, was not covered by this agreement. She thought that perhaps she would make a trip to Hong Kong when her daughter, who had become an actress with the Shanghai Film Studio, returned from northern China where her group was performing. However, when Meiping returned, the Cultural Revolution (involving the looting by the Red Guards) had been started by Chairman Mao. Nien Cheng felt that it would be risky to ask for permission to travel when this political campaign was in full swing.

Early one morning around 8 A.M. in spring 1966, Nien Cheng was visited by two men, formerly with Shell. Treating her in a rude manner, they announced that they had come to take her to a meeting that all former members of Shell had to attend. All too often people who were taken to meetings during political campaigns never came back. Nien Cheng's servants looked worried, but she tried to reassure them by saying she would be back for lunch.

The meeting was held in a large room at a technical school. Nien Cheng was ushered to a seat in the second row. None of the other members of the senior staff from Shell greeted her. Many looked troubled. Finally, a person representing the Communist party entered the room and began a three-hour talk about the evils of international corporations like Shell and capitalists like Tao Feng. (Tao Feng had been a chief accountant for Shell and had a son in the party who had been given special opportunities for study abroad.) Nien Cheng was surprised to see that this man had been picked out as the target, since she knew that he must have passed party scrutiny when his son was given these privileges. Sessions of this type were called "struggle" meetings, and it was the first Nien Cheng had seen.

She was able to get home for lunch, though the men that had brought her tried to force her to stay at the school for lunch so that she would not be late for the afternoon session. After lunch, Tao Feng was brought into the meeting with a white dunce cap on his head. He was required to stand on a chair. He looked thin and fearful. Gone was the self-confidence that Nien Cheng remembered he had had in the past. People began to shout slogans like "Down with Tao Feng!" Nien Cheng was surprised to see that Tao Feng joined in and later confessed to all of which he was accused. She thought that he looked exhausted and was close to physical collapse. Instead of being frightened, Nien Cheng thought that Tao Feng was foolish to have admitted the charges against him.

After the meeting, the man who had run it spoke to Nien and asked her what she had thought of the event. She inquired who had authorized it and was told that it was the committee in charge of the Proletarian Cultural Revolution in Shanghai. He then told her that she should copy Tao Feng and try to reform. Nien Cheng replied that she was not aware of any wrongdoing on her part.

After that session, there were several more in which officials met with Nien Cheng and asked her about her work at Shell and the many foreign friends she had. Her daughter, friends, and even her servants tried to warn her of the danger she was in with this attention focused on her. One of her late husband's friends, Mr. Hu, came to call on her to see how she was doing. Mr. Hu had been head of a factory but was now working as a laborer. He thought it was safer to be in a lowly position after being considered a capitalist. He told her that it had been his policy never to give a false confession no matter how great the pressure to do so.

Nien Cheng certainly was being invited to make a confession of past misbehavior. She felt that the men who met with her were stalling for time. Later she would learn that many of the lesser officials were uncertain about the Cultural Revolution, because this political movement was at the heart of a power struggle between certain followers of Chairman Mao Zedong and the more moderate faction headed by Liu Shaoqi, chairman of the Chinese republic from 1959 to 1969, and Deng Xiaoping, chairman of the party's advisory commission and military commission.

As the Cultural Revolution grew in size and the bands of young people that made up the Red Guards roamed the streets, life in Shanghai became even more chaotic. Nien Cheng had to go out to take care of some bank deposits that were past maturity date. Her servants warned her to dress in old clothes and wear a straw hat that her daughter had brought back from the countryside. Nien was glad that she had, because on the streets she saw Red Guards seizing people regardless of their class status and cutting off their hair or cutting the legs of their pants if they did not approve of how they looked. Even worse, she saw a man who was being led by a rope. He fell down from exhaustion and was beaten and jumped on.

Nien Cheng went into the bank and cashed a deposit for six thousand yuan (about twenty-four hundred dollars) that had reached maturity. She decided to give the six thousand to her servants immediately.

She set aside four hundred yuan in an envelope for her part-time gardener and gave the rest to the three full-time servants to divide among themselves as they thought best, because these people had been with her family for a long time. She told them that they could leave her any time if they were afraid. She said she would try to give them more after the Cultural Revolution was over, if she were financially able to do so. There was nothing more that she could do except to wait and see how she would fare in the Cultural Revolution.

In October 1966, old men and boys stand amid the rubble
of a Buddhist temple in a suburb of Beijing. The Red
Guard had entered this temple and ransacked it. Statuary
was damaged and broken and the Guards posted signs
on the temple walls.

Chapter 3

ARREST AND PRISON

The morning after the revolutionary action of the Red Guards, Nien Cheng sat in her house surveying the damage. All her books except those of Mao Zedong had been burned. She could not find her knitting or sewing, her pen, or any untorn paper. The radios had been taken. When her servant brought her the afternoon paper, the news praised the Red Guards as "little revolutionary generals" and warned against the capitalist class.

Nien Cheng was concerned for the safety of her servants and urged them to leave. They all wanted to stay. The cook told her that it was not safe for her to go to the market and buy food. He said that since he had a son in the army and the Communist party, it would be all right for him to stay until he was ordered to leave.

However, Nien Cheng was worried about Cheng-Ma, who had been with the family for years. Nien Cheng wrote to the daughter of Cheng-Ma telling her to come from the province where she lived to get her mother. When Cheng-Ma had to part, she tried to give Nien Cheng a warm sweater that she had knitted for her. The Red Guards would not let Cheng-Ma give the sweater to Nien Cheng. Nien Cheng was deeply touched by the loyalty of those who had worked for her.

The news that Meiping and others brought into the house continued to be frightening. A friend of Meiping's came to their house and suggested that Nien Cheng take Meiping and try to escape to Hong Kong, which was outside Red China. There Nien Cheng could count on help from her foreign friends. There was no hope for anyone in Communist China considered to be in the capitalist class. Nien Cheng thought that it was too late to leave. The penalty for trying to escape was ten to twenty years in prison. Because of the unrest in the country, the friend thought that they could get to Hong Kong. Later Nien Cheng learned that the friend had tried to leave, but had been turned back at the border. Finally, by swimming to the nearby Portuguese colony of Macao, he was able to get to Hong Kong.

When the Red Guards came again, they ordered Nien Cheng to kneel. One Guard hit her on the back and another on the back of her knees, forcing her to kneel. They left a girl with a whip to guard her. The girl demonstrated her prowess with the whip by swinging it back and forth over the head of Nien Cheng.

Then a group calling themselves the Proletarian Revolutionaries entered the house and asked Nien Cheng for her gold and weapons. Since firearms in a home had been illegal since 1949, it seemed farfetched to think that in 1966 some could still be around. They cut open mattresses and upholstery, removed tiles from the walls of the bathrooms, and even though it was dark, dug up the garden. After hours of searching without finding gold or weapons, the group was in a very hostile mood.

One of the men raised his arm to strike Nien Cheng. Meiping's cat, Fluffy, sank his teeth into the man's leg. The man howled in pain and tried to shake off the cat. Fluffy streaked out the door. The men ran after the cat, but he climbed into a magnolia tree out of reach of his pursuers. The Revolutionaries now accused Nien Cheng of keeping a wild animal and ordering the cat to attack. They shoved Nien Cheng back into the dining room and locked her in. One of the servants whispered that the cook had gone to warn Meiping not to return home that evening.

Then the Red Guards returned and confronted the Revolutionaries with shouting, then fighting. Sometime after daybreak, Nien Cheng was let out of the dining room and given water and food. She was ordered to help pack her things. Nien Cheng did so eagerly because she thought that when her things were packed, the Revolutionaries would leave. She was to be disappointed. One of the Revolutionaries was ordered to remain inside. Nien Cheng was placed under house arrest with Red Guards to watch her. She asked to see a written order, but she was told that she should be grateful not to go outside where she would be beaten to death because of the full-scale revolution going on.

While Meiping was allowed to keep her room, Nien Cheng was not permitted to talk with her daughter. Meiping had to stay more nights at her film studio, taking part in the activities of the Cultural Revolution. When Meiping did get home, Nien Cheng tried to push her door open to look at her daughter when she knew Meiping was coming up the stairs. When Nien Cheng was allowed to go out in the garden for exercise, she would find notes from her daughter crumpled into a small ball. Sometimes the notes would disintegrate in the rain before Nien Cheng went out. However, the messages of "I love you, Mom," and "Take care of yourself" were a great boost to Nien Cheng's morale.

Lao-zhao, the servant allowed to stay and cook for Nien Cheng, was not supposed to talk directly with her. However, he could strike up a conversation with the Red Guard assigned to watch them. Through these conversations and copies of the *Red Guard News* that were lying around, Nien Cheng learned what was going on in the outside world. Teachers were beaten. Different political factions supported different groups of Red Guards that would compete with each other in violence.

Children of "capitalist" families were singled out for abuse. A country that was supposed to be pledged to equality was making circumstances of birth a basis for judging different classes of people. Meiping was soon the target of this attitude. She was removed from the rank of the "masses" and was considered a class enemy who had to write confessions and self-criticisms. Lao-zhao reported to the Red Guard that he had seen Meiping and that she was looking well and was writing self-criticism. The servant asked why Meiping should be doing this because she was a member of the Communist Youth League and had always received citations of merit. The Guard replied that of course Meiping should be writing a self-criticism because of her family background, that she was probably a "radish" anyhow—red on the outside but white on the inside. (Red was the color identified with the Communists.) The Guard reported that the Communist Youth League was disbanded because the leader, Hu Yaobang, was no longer in favor and had been purged. (After the Cultural Revolution came to an end when Chairman Mao died in September 1976, Hu was rehabilitated and steadily rose to become chairman of the Communist party in 1981.)

Soon after, a Guard took Meiping's belongings to the film studio where she had to stay. Nien Cheng was depressed over this change of events, fearing for her daughter, and sorry to miss even the possibility of seeing her.

Late in the afternoon of September 27, Nien Cheng was escorted to a school building in which "struggle" meetings were held. These sessions were designed to break people's will and get them to confess to some misdeed. Nien Cheng was led into a room and told to stand in the center with a Red Guard on either side. The seats placed in an irregular circle were filled with Red Guards and former Shell employees.

The leader of the meeting then gave a history of Nien Cheng and her family, going back more than one hundred years. The account was full of inaccuracies and was designed to make Nien Cheng appear to be a foreign spy. Then a Red Guard stood up to tell of the luxuries in her home. Another described her efforts to undermine their activities by trying to save the "old culture." A revolutionary described the attack of her "wild animal," Fluffy.

Then the former Shell employees were called to give evidence. They appeared frightened and did not look at Nien Cheng. They told of files to which only she and the British manager had access. They reported that whenever she and the manager rode in the same car, the manager always permitted her to get in first. No Chinese senior executive would let a female assistant get in first. She therefore must have been very important to the British imperialists. She and her husband were said to have always sided with the British against the Chinese.

Although the evening wore on, no one left this struggle meeting that exposed an "international spy." Later Nien Cheng learned that the meeting had been postponed several times in the hopes of getting her daughter to denounce her. Meiping refused, and because the revolutionaries in Shanghai wanted some results to celebrate on October 1—National Day—they decided to go ahead with the meeting without the daughter's participation.

The leader called on Nien Cheng to confess. She replied: "I have never done anything against the Chinese people and government. The Shell office was here because the Chinese government wanted it to be here."[1] Although she spoke these words loudly, she doubted that anyone in the room could hear a complete sentence because she was interrupted by cries of "Confess!" and "Dirty spy!" People crowded around her and pushed her. There was no way that she could reason with this crowd.

Finally the leader said that Nien Cheng was guilty. He said they could give her the death sentence for her actions, but they wanted to give her the chance to confess. She stood silently, feeling sad rather than hostile that there was no way that she could get the truth across to these people.

She was shown a pair of handcuffs and led outside. Again Nien Cheng was challenged to confess. She recited the Twenty-third Psalm to herself. She felt freer of fear than she had at any time during the meeting. Although she was standing next to the police vehicle, she did not respond. The police pulled her arms behind her and put on the handcuffs.

Just then Nien Cheng heard the voice of a girl: "Confess! Confess quickly! They are going to take you to prison!" Nien Cheng turned and saw the speaker. It was the girl who had been at the desk with her jewelry—now trying to help her. The girl was drawn back by an older woman and taken into the school building. Nien Cheng was bundled into the police jeep and whisked through the streets of Shanghai.

After a siren-blaring ride, the jeep stopped at the gates of Number One Detention House. The gates were guarded by armed sentries. This place was the primary prison for political prisoners and had housed Roman Catholic bishops, Kuomintang officials, industrialists, writers and artists, and, under past regimes, Communists.

Nien Cheng was led into the main building and told by a female guard to undress. Her clothes were searched and then given back to her—except for her brassiere. It was considered a bad Western form of dress. The envelope with the four hundred yuan that she had intended to give to the gardener was found in her pocket and was deposited for her with the prison authorities. She was fingerprinted and mug-shot pictures were taken. The guard assigned her number 1806. She would be known by this number instead of her name.

Number 1806 was given a sheet of prison regulations to read. First, prisoners had to study the books of Mao Zedong daily to reform their thinking. Second, they must confess their crimes and denounce others. Third, they must report to the guards any infringement of rules by prisoners in the same cell. The rest of the regulations dealt with daily life in the detention house.

Next Nien Cheng was led to the women's building and down the long prison corridor that was to figure in her nightmares over the years. The guard unbolted the lock on a cell, put Nien

Cheng in, and told her to go to sleep. Nien Cheng asked to use the toilet. The guard pointed to a cement fixture in the corner of the room. The guard said she would lend Nien Cheng some toilet paper. The same number of sheets would have to be given back when Nien Cheng received her supply.

Cobwebs and a single dirty light bulb hung from the ceiling. The walls were yellowed whitewash streaked with dust. In places the cement floor was black with dampness. The only pieces of furniture were three narrow beds of rough wooden planks, one against the wall and two stacked one on top of the other.

When Nien Cheng stood on tiptoes and opened the dirty window, a shower of paint chips and dust came down on top of her. She had to endure the dirt on the bed and the mosquitoes that bit her badly. She could not control the light, but just before dawn, the light was shut off. This was the time of day when Nien Cheng felt the greatest sense of dignity and freedom from the gaze of the guards.

According to Nien Cheng: "Never in my life had I been in or even imagined a place so primitive and filthy."[2] Yet she hoped that because of her imprisonment, some of the pressure to denounce her had been removed from her daughter.

Activity helped Nien Cheng. She requested a broom and cleaned her cell. She made rice paste from some of her food and pasted sheets of toilet paper on a part of the dirty wall she faced in bed. She bought thread. On Sundays she could get a

41

needle from the guard. She sewed together toilet paper sheets to form a cover for the wash basin she was allowed to buy with the money that had been deposited for her. She also made an eyeshade to block out the glare from the bulb. The clothes and bedding from her home were brought to her, but they contained no note from her daughter, though she searched hopefully for it. The food—a watery rice porridge with a few strips of pickled vegetables—was so bad that she had a hard time swallowing it.

Often Nien Cheng asked to see a "responsible person" (the name that the Communists used instead of a title). She wanted to clear up the misunderstanding that had landed her in the detention house. The guards replied that she was there because she had committed a crime and should confess. When she responded that she had not committed any crime, she was told: "Your being here proves you have committed a crime."[3] When she asked to study the law books to see what crime she had committed, the guard told her that she was talking like a capitalist intellectual. Instead, he announced: "We go by the teachings of our Great Leader Chairman Mao. His words are our criteria. If he says a certain type of person is guilty and you belong to that type, then you are guilty. It's much simpler than depending on a lawbook."[4]

Chapter 4

INTERROGATION

Late in November the northwest wind brought chilly temperatures. Nien Cheng woke up with a bad cold and a headache. She drank the warm watery rice, but had to return the dry rice and cabbage that was served at noon. That evening a guard opened the small window in her cell door and said to her: "You have been crying."[1] The guard said that Nien Cheng was not used to the prison conditions and missed her daughter. The guard urged her to have a correct attitude and be repentant.

Nien Cheng protested that she just had a cold and asked for an aspirin. However, the guards must have assumed that she was at a weak point. She was finally called for interrogation—two months after being in the detention house. She was told to bring her book of Chairman Mao's quotations. She was led to a narrow, dark room with only a small window high on the wall that she faced. In front of her were two men dressed in the baggy blue cotton Maoist uniform that most men wore. The men were seated behind a wooden counter. There was a heavy wooden chair for the person to be interrogated. One of the men ordered her to read one of the quotations from Mao's book and then to sit down. As she did so, she noticed that the door behind her had a small window. She assumed that the proceedings were being observed from the corridor. She was disappointed because it seemed that the real authority was out of the room and the men in front of her were just the subordinates.

The men began by asking her if she knew where she was. Nien Cheng replied that she assumed it was some kind of prison. The men told her that she was there because she had committed a crime against the people's government. She replied that there must have been some mistake and challenged them to produce evidence. The men said that the government would rather give her the chance to earn lenient treatment by confessing and by incriminating others. Nien Cheng responded that she had nothing to confess. Her interrogators replied that if she was not ready to confess then, they could wait. They also said she would not last five years in prison, that her health would break down and she would die, and that she would be begging for a chance to confess.

Nien Cheng quoted back one of Mao's sayings about not fearing hardship or death. She was told that quotation was only meant for soldiers. She countered that Marshal Lin Biao, head of the Red Army, had taught that all the teachings of Mao were applicable in all circumstances.

No concrete questions were being asked. She was not learning who was behind her imprisonment or why she was being held. Finally, she just let the men talk on without interruption. They warned her that she would not get out without changing her thinking. They reminded her that it would be very cold in her cell in the winter. They said that she must be wondering about her daughter. Finally, they gave her a roll of paper and ordered her to write her autobiography in chronological order, beginning with her family. She was to give the finished report to the guard and then she would be called again for interrogation.

As she went back to her cell, Nien Cheng puzzled over what she had learned from this encounter. She did not think that it was just her life-style that had resulted in her imprisonment. She knew of other women who lived comfortably who had not been seized. She knew that she had to be careful in writing her autobiography because her words could be twisted. She was aware of others who had been assigned this task more than once and then had had differences between the two accounts used against them.

After carefully considering how to protect herself, she wrote a short account in chronological order that she knew she could repeat if necessary. She turned it in to the guard the next day. The guard asked her if she was sure that she had included everything, because it was so short. Nien Cheng asked innocently: "Oh, is it too short? In any case, I did put everything in."[2]

When she was called the next day for further interrogation, she knew that the men would probably be unhappy with her autobiography. They were. They spoke sharply to her and criticized her writing. Nien Cheng asked them to tell her what they wanted to know, that it was not her intention to try to hide anything because she counted on her interrogators to clear her name and restore her reputation.

Then they asked her about two British spies and about a White Russian double agent who was a secretary to the Shell manager. She was shocked by their questions. Her attempt to reply was cut short by the interrogators, who told her to go back to her cell and think about it. She would be given a chance to confess in the afternoon.

The guards watched her very carefully to see how she was behaving, whether or not she ate her noon meal, whether she was upset. Nien Cheng knew that she must act normally—otherwise she would be thought guilty.

In the afternoon session, she was questioned about her relationship with the spies. She realized that for some reason, it was important to these men to identify her as a "spy." For most prisoners, any charge was enough to get them sent away to a labor camp as punishment. Nien Cheng had always felt secure because she had been in no position, working with a foreign company, to know any "state secrets." She had been careful never to ask any questions about sensitive subjects. Now she felt frightened—not because she was guilty but because she wondered whether she would be equal to the task of defending herself.

She waited for further interrogation sessions, but none

came. She sensed a tension among the guards. The newspaper given to the prisoners for indoctrination stopped coming. While out in the exercise yard of the prison, Nien Cheng heard a mob outside the walls. A prisoner whispered loud enough for all to hear: "It's probably the Red Guards trying to get in to rescue their comrades imprisoned by the municipal government!"[3] Gunshots were fired. The sound of the mob came from farther away. The prison guards must have been shaken by the attempt of the Red Guards to break in.

That Christmas Eve, Nien Cheng listened as a beautiful soprano voice from somewhere upstairs began singing "Silent Night" in Chinese. The singer must have been a professional musician who was out of favor with the Maoists. Everyone was very quiet listening to the song. Just as it finished, the guards rushed in to find out who was singing, but none of the prisoners told them.

On January 4, the prisoners were ordered to listen to an important announcement over the loudspeaker. The Red Guards had seized power from the existing government in Shanghai. All government departments were being reorganized including the Public Security Bureau responsible for the detention house. Nien Cheng realized that this process meant that her case would not be resolved quickly.

Above: Members of the Red Guard hold booklets that contain the writings of Mao Zedong. Some have opened the booklet to display a portrait of Mao. Below: Carrying their belongings on their backs, young Red Guards march on a street in Beijing in 1966.

Above: Two men considered to be against Mao are forced to wear placards around their necks that denounce them and they are driven through the streets to be ridiculed. Below: Chinese Premier Zhou Enlai addresses a rally in Beijing stadium in 1967.

Above: In October 1987 Nien Cheng was awarded the first
Humanitarian Award from Slippery Rock University in
Pennsylvania. To honor Meiping, Nien Cheng has established
an annual scholarship at Slippery Rock in her daughter's
name. Below: Nien Cheng's photos of her husband Kang-chi
and her daughter Meiping.

Above: Nien Cheng became an American citizen in 1988. Below: Nien Cheng in her Washington, D.C., apartment in 1992.

In May 1989 jubilant Chinese students stage a pro-democracy
march (above) to Tiananmen Square in central Beijing
to begin a sit-in. Troops and tanks stormed the square
on June 4 and killed and injured many of the
students (below).

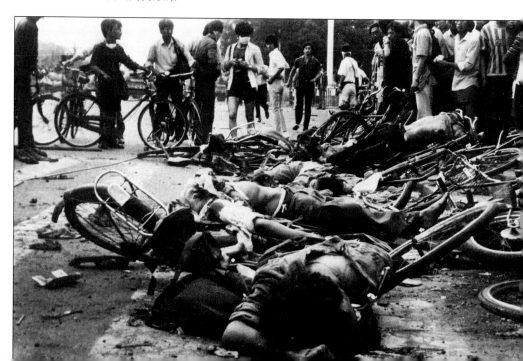

Left: After becoming a U.S. citizen in 1988, Nien Cheng posed in front of the Statue of Liberty. Below: On May 30, 1989 in Tiananmen Square, Chinese students unveiled a replica of the Statue of Liberty they named "The Goddess of Democracy."

During the Cultural Revolution, people who were singled out by the Red Guard were ridiculed in public. These counterrevolutionary Chinese were forced to wear dunce caps and were on display in Beijing in 1967.

Chapter 5

THE HOSPITAL

During her second winter in the detention house, Nien Cheng again developed a bad cold that was to turn into serious bronchitis. One night when she was unable to sleep because of her coughing and sneezing, she heard the window in the door of her cell being opened. The guard called her over. She was surprised to find that it was her former interrogator, who now brought a thermos of hot water to fill her mug. It had been more than a year since she had been interrogated, and she asked when he was going to clarify her case. He replied that the revolutionaries would call her when they were ready. Apparently, he was no longer in charge of her case and was only a guard now. He talked to another man, whom he addressed as Director Liang—the person formerly in charge but now also just a guard.

Nien Cheng wondered what these men now thought about the work of the detention house, because they were offering hot water to a prisoner to soothe her throat. Were the revolutionaries driving away the people who had formerly supported them? What was going on in the minds of the party cadres, now that they were subject to revolutionary action?

Treatment at the detention house under the new leadership

became even harsher. Now there were to be two meals instead of three—and with poorer food. Lists of prisoners to be put to death because they had not confessed were read over the loudspeaker. Then they read those who were to receive lenient treatment because they had admitted their guilt and had incriminated others.

Not long after the loudspeaker was turned off, Nien Cheng heard footsteps approaching her cell. The shutter of the window on her cell door was opened and she was asked why she had not confessed. She replied that she was not guilty. She was told that she was a spy and could be shot if she did not confess. Her cell was unlocked, and she was ordered to step out. One of the men was dressed in the uniform of an air force officer.

Nien Cheng had taken only a couple of steps to follow the officer down the corridor, when a commotion broke out in the cell above. She was shoved back in her cell, while the authorities answered the call from above for help. Apparently one of the prisoners there had tried to commit suicide by hitting her head against the cement toilet. The men never came back for Nien Cheng. She wondered what would have happened to her if they had not been interrupted.

Under the new prison administration, interrogation consisted of lectures and threats—but usually no answers to questions were expected. Searches of the cells were frequent.

Nien Cheng caught another cold and had a high fever. She

asked to see the doctor, but was told that he had been sent away to be reeducated and given hard labor. Instead a country boy with no medical training had been assigned to treat the prisoners. He told Nien Cheng that she might have hepatitis! Anyone could tell from her symptoms that she had bronchitis — or even pneumonia. When her fever increased and she was barely conscious, she was taken to the hospital.

Nien Cheng was horrified at the dirty and smelly waiting room at the hospital. It was filled with starved-looking people in ragged clothes. They looked as if they were suffering real pain. When the nurse called out "1806," Nien Cheng followed her into the examining room. Here male and female patients had to undress without the privacy that always had been the rule in Chinese hospitals. Nien Cheng thought that these conditions were present because it was a prison hospital. But later she was to learn that all Shanghai hospitals had fallen to similar low standards. Fortunately, Nien Cheng only had to have her temperature taken before the doctor said to the guard that the prisoner had better stay at the hospital for a few days.

The guard took Nien Cheng to the assigned ward. She was cautioned not to discuss her case with anyone. The prisoner was turned over to a labor reform woman — someone who had been sentenced to this kind of labor. Nien Cheng was instructed to lie down on the bed — a real bed, not just the wooden planks that she had in the cell. Then she lost consciousness. Six days later she regained consciousness and was disconnected from intravenous tubes. That evening she feasted on a meal of rice, vegetables, and even a six-inch yellow fish.

After the soldier guarding the ward locked up the unit, one of the other patients came over to talk with Nien Cheng. This patient, who suffered from tuberculosis, told her that the doctor had been afraid that Nien Cheng might die. The patient reported that the doctor was a graduate of a medical school in the United States. The doctor had left a good job there to return to China when the government had called for patriotic Chinese to come back to help the people. Unfortunately the doctor had a habit of speaking frankly, so she ended up in prison. After she was released, she volunteered to come back and work in the prison hospital. Nien Cheng felt that there was something saintly in the way that this doctor cared for and talked with the patients.

Gradually, Nien Cheng regained her strength. She received medicine and good food. The labor reform woman on the unit was so professionally competent that Nien Cheng decided that she must have been a nurse. Although they did not speak with each other, Nien Cheng noticed that the woman did not have good food or warm clothing. Nien Cheng motioned for her to take a sweater. She did not talk for fear that the guard outside would hear. The woman refused after looking nervously in the direction of the guard.

Soon, Nien Cheng was well enough to be returned to the Number One Detention House.

Chapter 6

BACK TO THE DETENTION HOUSE

Nien Cheng continued to suffer from health problems because of the lack of good food, sunshine, and fresh air. She found it more difficult to concentrate and think logically. Handfuls of her hair fell out. Her gums bled. She lost weight. Often she had difficulty swallowing, even though she was very hungry. She felt discouraged and was frightened that she might die before her case was resolved.

One day when her hands shook, her heart beat wildly, and her legs became unsteady, she knew that she would have to do something. She had to help herself physically and mentally. She planned a series of exercises that would move every part of her body. These she did twice a day. At first this workout exhausted her. She had to be careful not to let the guards see her. It was forbidden to exercise in the cell, except to walk after meals. To exercise her mind, she memorized some of Mao's essays that she thought she might be able to use in her defense. Also, she tried to remember some of the Tang Dynasty poetry that she had memorized in school.

Whenever she felt too depressed, she would try to release her anger by picking a verbal fight with the guards. She felt that these arguments were enjoyed by the other prisoners, just as their defiance strengthened her. Also, it would help her get out of the depression that was affecting her sleeping and eating. Of course, the risk was that sometimes the guards beat and kicked her.

Nien Cheng's health seemed to be getting better. But a new physical problem struck her. She began to lose an unusually large amount of blood during her menstrual periods. Then she began hemorrhaging every ten days or so for a period of several days. She tried to keep this problem secret because she feared the medical treatment she might receive at the detention house.

When the guards discovered that she was bleeding, they reported her condition. Fortunately the young doctor, not the soldier from the country, was back on the job at the prison. He told Nien Cheng that she might just be going through her menopause, the end of her menstrual periods, or she might have some kind of growth. The doctor would have liked to have had her examined by a gynecologist, but the prison hospital did not have this type of doctor. He gave Nien Cheng some injections to stop the bleeding but left her with the fear that she might have cancer.

Two years after her last interrogation, on a cold day in January 1969, Nien Cheng was surprised when someone was moved into her cell. She was glad to have some human company, but thought it strange that someone would be placed with her now. There did not appear to be many new people being brought to the detention house. Soon the woman was asking her questions about prison life. Nien Cheng suspected from her pale face, her thin body, and her frightened expression that the woman had been in prison for some time. When her new roommate asked questions that could have gotten them both into a great deal of trouble, Nien Cheng warned her that they were not allowed to talk with each other. When the roommate persisted and the guards did nothing to stop her, Nien Cheng felt sure that a trap had been set for her. A spy was in her cell.

On the fourth day they were together, the roommate was called out for interrogation but did not return to the cell. That evening, the loudspeaker broadcast the announcement that the roommate had been given the death sentence, to be carried out immediately because she was a spy for the Kuomintang. Because she had not confessed and sought lenient treatment, she would be crushed to powder by the iron fist of the Dictatorship of the Proletariat.

A guard had observed Nien Cheng during this announcement. Nien Cheng realized that she had to be careful not to show nervousness that might be interpreted as guilt. The guard said that Nien Cheng should consider the fate of the roommate in connection with her own case. Nien Cheng replied that if the roommate was a spy she deserved to die, but that Nien Cheng was not a spy and that she expected the People's Government to clarify her case and fully rehabilitate her.

That night when the guards came to get the possessions and quilt of the roommate, Nien Cheng felt certain that the woman had not been killed but needed the quilt that night to keep warm. One of the guards slapped and kicked Nien Cheng while insulting and threatening her.

The next morning Nien Cheng was called for interrogation — this time in front of five men. They told her that she could not hope to escape punishment any more than Liu Shaoqi. He had been Mao's principal deputy and occupied the position of chairman of the republic, but had been toppled by the more radical group in the party. Pretending to be stupid, Nien Cheng said that she had always had the greatest respect for Liu Shaoqi and was not sure that he was guilty of the charges against him.

This defense of a leader out of favor brought an outburst from the five interrogators, although several of them looked at her with curiosity and amusement. Why, if she were opposed to the Communist party, would she rally to the support of their deposed leader?

At one point when Nien Cheng was accused of not supporting the Communist party, she left her chair, marched to the table in front of the interrogators, and banged on it for emphasis. All five men stood up, and the soldier took his gun out of his holster and pointed it at her. She told him to shoot her if they had evidence to prove her guilty.

When the head interrogator told her to return to her chair, the session continued. He said: "We want you to confess because others are involved. You yourself are of no importance. We couldn't care less whether you are dead or alive."[1]

It dawned on Nien Cheng that she was but a pawn between factions in the party. Although she had never met the party leaders and they did not know her, her confession that she was a spy would hurt the Communist leaders who had authorized foreign companies to operate in China. By refusing to confess, she was helping some unknown leader in the Communist party. Was it possible that the party was after Prime Minister Zhou Enlai, who had personally approved the trip that she and her husband had made to Europe? That idea seemed as improbable as the downfall of Liu Shaoqi. But that had actually happened.

To test her theory, Nien Cheng decided to try her stupid-innocence approach with another defense of Liu Shaoqi. Immediately, she was told to stop. She could not resist a final dig: "Of course I do not dare to defend Liu Shaoqi if he is really guilty. But I do wonder if the material on which the Central Committee based its judgment was really reliable. You know how people can easily be frightened into making false confessions. I suppose it happens all the time."[2]

Later after Mao's death in 1976, China would learn that the evidence against Liu Shaoqi had been obtained through torture of Liu's associates. However, the fear on the faces of the five interrogators at her comment indicated that even at that time, party members suspected that the evidence was false.

What happened to Nien Cheng the rest of that day was a

surprising break from the usual practices of the guards. Food had been kept warm for her. She was given hot water when she returned to her cell. A doctor had been ordered without her request to look at her ankle where the guard had kicked her the night before. Why were these considerations shown to her? Was it her defense of Liu Shaoqi, or was the Maoist faction trying to soften her up with this kindness?

The strain of that day was too much for her body. That night she had a severe hemorrhage that sent her back to the hospital. She was disappointed that the interrogation that had just begun in earnest was to be interrupted. She was afraid that she might have cancer after all. She did not want to die before her case was cleared up because her daughter then would be under suspicion. Besides, she wanted so very much to see Meiping again.

The doctor was able to stop the hemorrhaging with injections, but could not arrange for Nien Cheng to see a gynecologist. However, the doctor did order rice twice a day and some meat. The doctor sent Nien Cheng back to the detention house with the advice to eat everything she could and to try to be optimistic. With tears in her eyes, the doctor said softly: "May God bless you!"[3]

Back at the detention house, the doctor there gave Nien Cheng permission to buy vitamin pills with the money she had on deposit. The Maoist guards showed their displeasure of her extra food and medicine by shouting at her or shoving, pinching, and kicking her. The guards supporting Liu Shaoqi sometimes brought her glucose powder along with the vitamin pills.

The interrogations continued. Nien Cheng was asked to write a confession each day. She always wrote the same thing. Finally they tried something new. She was driven to a struggle meeting, like the one that had been held for the former chief accountant for Shell. Handcuffed, she was dragged into the meeting room by the guards and half thrown to the floor where she was to sit. A man behind her held his hand on her head so that she could not look around.

The program consisted of persons who had been employed by Shell telling about the spying at the company. Nien Cheng thought that it was absurd and could be believed only by someone who had no idea of anything outside China. When Tao, the former accountant stood up, he spoke of how sorry he was for what he had done and how he wanted to confess to get lenient treatment. He said that he had been a spy because of Nien Cheng and her husband and that she had offered him money if he would not confess.

Nien Cheng knew that her denial or argument would be ignored, but she wanted to stop the meeting somehow. She threw back her head and laughed uproariously. This act was so surprising that no one spoke at first. Then several men rushed at her and her head was pushed down again. The leader of the meeting shouted, "Why did you laugh?" Nien Cheng responded: "If you put on a comic play, you must expect the audience to laugh. It's the natural response."[4] The tense mood of the session had been broken. She was taken out while slogans were shouted against her.

No sooner was she back in the detention house than she was taken for interrogation. She fainted, probably from hunger. A doctor revived her. This time there were at least eight men present. They criticized her laughter and told her to confess. The next day in the interrogation session, she was accused of being unpatriotic for dancing with a foreigner. Nien Cheng turned the words around and pointed out how useful she must have been by making the foreigner unpatriotic. Her humor was not appreciated. During the next several days of interrogation she was forced to stand. She had to read over and over, for at least as long as seven hours, one letter that had been written by Chairman Mao.

Still Nien Cheng did not confess. The interrogations were used simply to try to find her guilty—not to determine the facts. Then, every few days, she was taken to struggle meetings in what was called "rotating struggle" during the spring of 1969. She was forced to listen to the angry accusations and often her body was abused. Still, she was not frightened by these meetings. She drew into herself, and she would not confess.

Chapter 7

HER BROTHER'S CONFESSION AND HER TORTURE

The warmer weather of spring 1969 brought relief from the cold, but Nien Cheng found that the dampness was causing her joints to become red and swollen with pain and stiffness. Her gums also were getting swollen and filled with blood. She had to press the blood out with her finger and rinse the salty food so that she could eat without pain and tasting blood. The doctor gave her sulfa drugs, but told her that there was no dental department at the prison.

A series of interrogation sessions gave her some hope that perhaps her case was being investigated seriously. She was asked about her relatives and friends, one by one, and was told to write long accounts telling of her contacts with each one. She knew that her accounts would be checked against those of the relatives and friends. When she was urged to provide evidence against someone, then she understood that that person was in trouble. She would try to write something about their loyalty to the Communists to help the person under investigation.

This practice of requiring people to testify against each other during the Mao Zedong rule was very destructive to friendships and family relationships. Even husbands and wives and parents and children had to be careful what they said in front of one another. Often people had to lie to guard themselves and their families. The only real protection was not to speak one's thoughts.

In Nien Cheng's interrogations, she could often guess which of her relatives or friends was under pressure to supply information against her. Toward the end of 1969, she was told to confess that she was a supporter of the Kuomintang. Since she was the widow of a former diplomatic officer of the Kuomintang—the government before the Communists—she was not surprised at the demand. However, she continued to deny any support for the Kuomintang since she and her husband had elected to stay in China when the Communists came to power.

Nien Cheng was asked whether she had ever had her picture taken in front of the Kuomintang flag. Thinking that her questioners might be referring to something from the time she was in Australia before the Communists came to power, she replied that she might have but she couldn't remember. The interrogators inquired about a photograph after the Communists came to power. Nien Cheng could not imagine what they were talking about. She asked how there could be a Kuomintang flag for a picture at that time and denied that she had such a picture. Her interrogators told her that someone had confessed that she had, and she had better confess or she would miss the chance for lenient treatment.

Nien Cheng was sent back to her cell to think over the matter. For three weeks she was called every two or three days to talk about this subject. The guard withheld the sulfa drug that she needed for her gums. She was weak, in pain, and finding it difficult to think straight. After she fainted because of lack of food and was taken to the hospital, the sulfa drugs were made available to her again.

Each time she was called for interrogation, she was asked about the Kuomintang and the flag. Finally, they gave her the clue to think back to 1962. The only thing she could recall in 1962 was her mother's death. As the eldest child, she had arranged the funeral. With great difficulty and after a sizable contribution to the Buddhist Research Institute in Nanjing, she had been able to get several monks to recite the *sutras*, the Buddhist scriptures, at her mother's funeral. Also, she had arranged, according to Chinese custom, to have all her mother's children listed on the tombstone — even the names of the two sisters now in America.

Although the interrogators were critical of her bowing to religious superstition and recognizing her foreign sisters, what they really zeroed in on was the Kuomintang flag. They said that after the burial the family had gone to the Sun Yatsen Memorial to have their photograph taken in front of the Kuomintang flag to pledge their loyalty to the Kuomintang government in Taiwan.

Nien Cheng was astounded. She denied that the family had

gone to the memorial. They had been so tired that they had gone straight home. Moreover, she doubted that there was any Kuomintang flag at the memorial. Had they checked? Besides, a photograph certainly would not impress the Kuomintang government with their loyalty when the family had elected to stay in China when the Communists took power. She suggested that the interrogators ask the other members of her family.

They replied that they had already done so. Her brother at first denied everything. But then he had told his questioners that Nien Cheng had suggested that they go to the Sun Yatsen Memorial and that her camera had been used to take the picture. He told them that she had sent him a copy of it. When Nien Cheng heard this, she became concerned for her brother and wondered what had been done to him to force such a story from him. She knew that he was not normally stupid or disloyal. She urged her interrogators to go to Nanjing and see if there was a Kuomintang flag. Since she was not called again, she assumed they had done so and found no flag.

After her release from prison, Nien Cheng tried to get in touch with her brother, but he refused to correspond with her. Her Western contacts made her dangerous. After Mao died, however, her brother invited her to visit in Beijing. She did not bring up the subject of the photograph, but he asked about it. She told him that she had sent a picture of their mother in 1962, but that was all. He said that his interrogators had told him over and over about the photo with the flag until it seemed to him that the photo had been taken.

Her brother had been through much. He had once worked for a Kuomintang government official. In 1957, he was subjected to many struggle meetings. He was an economist for the Communists, but would not lie in his reports about conditions, so he was sent to the country to raise chickens. When he was successful at this task and when the people in the country came to him for advice, the local official wanted him sent away. He then became an English teacher. Finally at the end of his life, he was reinstated as a professor of economics.

The brother felt that it was useless to resist the pressures from the government. Only by going along with the Communists could one avoid getting hurt. His way was the opposite from Nien Cheng's defiance. She felt that he was disappointed in her for not being like the wise Chinese who "bend with the wind to survive the hurricane."[1]

After the matter of the Kuomintang flag had been dropped by her interrogators, Nien Cheng was not called for more sessions. She had the impression that she might be released after her activities had been examined, so she was depressed that there was no further action in her case.

The winter of 1969-70 was miserable for Nien Cheng. There was heavy snow, intense cold, and always the physical pain. Often the goods that she was allowed to buy were not available. The shortages seemed to be affecting the guards as well.

She guessed the country was going through another economic crisis. In the spring, another bout with pneumonia sent her to the hospital again. After a slow recovery, she returned to the detention house. She felt renewed after having survived another dangerous crisis.

Now the Communists were tightening their control in the country. From within the prison it was harder to piece together what was going on outside. When Nien Cheng realized that one of the radical leaders was no longer listed among the highest ranking government officials and when there were criticisms in the newspaper of a "fake Marxist," she realized another of the leaders had been eliminated. Also, China seemed to be moving in the direction of winning diplomatic recognition from Western countries. Did this mean that the power of Prime Minister Zhou Enlai was increasing, while that of Lin Biao and the military was decreasing?

Nien Cheng was surprised to be called to the interrogation room one afternoon in January 1971. There she found five guards. They shouted at her and began pushing her around. They shoved her back and forth between them as though she were a ball in a game. When she lost her balance, one male guard picked her up by the lapels of her padded jacket and gave her a shove against the wall. She was bounced against the wall several times. Nien Cheng vomited onto his hands and cuffs. He shoved her into the chair. Then the others struck her cheeks and pulled her hair.

They kept asking, "Are you going to confess?" Nien Cheng thought: "It seemed that they really thought I would change my mind simply because they had beaten me up. But then, people who resort to brutality must believe in the power of brutality. It seemed to me that these guards at the detention house were rather stupid not to know me better after watching me day and night for so many years. I knew, however, that they were merely carrying out someone else's orders."[2]

When Nien Cheng remained silent, one of the guards placed her arms around the back of the chair. Another put a pair of handcuffs on her. A third asked again whether she would confess or did she want more punishment. Nien Cheng said that she had done nothing wrong and had nothing to confess. In response, one of the guards tightened the handcuffs so that they fit snugly around her wrists.

Nien Cheng was led away. This time she was placed in a room only about five feet square. It was without a window and was dark. She was left there. Every once in a while, guards came into the corridor outside this room to ask Nien Cheng if she were going to confess.

Her hands felt hot and stiff. Her head ached. Nien Cheng tried to get some circulation into her legs. Finally she put her head on her knees and tried to rest. She prayed and tried to think of beautiful things to keep her mind occupied. As her fingers became swollen, she worried about whether she might lose her hands. She remembered the painting that she and her late husband had bought after World War II. It had been painted by a veteran who had lost his hands and held the paint brush with his toes.

When a guard came in the building, she asked to have the handcuffs loosened. But when she refused to confess, she was told that the handcuffs would not be removed until she did so. Nien Cheng told herself that she would just have to accept being crippled and stop worrying about her hands.

After being locked in the small cell for almost twenty-four hours without food or water, she was taken back to the interrogation room. Again they challenged her to confess. A year or so before, she would have argued with the guards. Now she was too ill and tired to say anything. Then she was taken back to her cell with the handcuffs still in place.

Now to drink water, she had to remove the cover of her mug with her teeth and tip the mug so that the water spilled into her mouth as she squatted down to table level. She had to refuse food because she did not know how she could eat it. There was no comfortable position in which to sleep, and her hands were hot from the swelling and pressure, even though it was so bitterly cold that she could see her breath. She had to get up to walk to keep warm, but then her hands hurt more.

After the third day without food, one of the older guards told her that she might starve to death if she did not figure out how she could eat. The guard said there was a way—that a spoon was there. Because the guard sounded sympathetic,

Nien Cheng asked again about having the handcuffs loosened, but the guard said that the key to the handcuffs was kept by a higher official.

Nien Cheng discovered that she could loosen the rice with a spoon held behind her and dump it out on a clean towel. Then she had to eat the rice off the towel without the use of her hands. Whenever she moved the handcuffs hurt her wrists, which now oozed blood and pus. Her feet also became swollen. Soon her physical condition began to affect her mind. She could no longer understand what the guards said to her. She could no longer get up to take the rice. She lay there going in and out of consciousness until she passed out.

When Nien Cheng came to, she was on the floor of her cell. The handcuffs had been removed. Her hands and her feet had swollen to an enormous size. The blisters on her feet made it nearly impossible for her to walk without pain. When she finally reached the window of her cell and asked for medical attention, she was told that none would be given. She was not allowed even to have bandages or an antiseptic to prevent infection.

When she finally was given some hot water, Nien Cheng cleaned the wounds on her wrists and feet carefully. She wanted to tear up an old pillowcase for bandages, but she could no longer reach her arms up to the clothesline where she had hung it before she had been called out of her cell.

When Nien Cheng was given her afternoon meal, she found

her container filled to the brim with rice and cabbage. Buried underneath were two hard-boiled eggs—a treat indeed. The woman from the kitchen, to prevent any thanks being given, grumbled that Nien Cheng was always so slow and she should give the tray to the guard on duty at night. When the night guard came to pick up the tray, she brought the newspaper. From the paper, Nien Cheng learned that eleven days had elapsed from the time she had been called to the interrogation room and the handcuffs had been put on.

Not long after that Nien Cheng was called to go out to the outdoor exercise yard. She asked to be excused because her feet were so painful, but the guards refused. She was taken to a different place than usual. She was ordered to start walking. Nien Cheng angrily replied that she could not walk, that her feet and hands were painful, and that blood and pus were coming out of the wounds. Instead of punishing her for her outburst, the guard seemed pleased. Nien Cheng was told to walk to the middle of the yard and to face the other way. Nien Cheng wondered what the guard did not want her to see. Turning her body slightly, she glimpsed three men in military overcoats leaving the guard stand. Were these the higher authorities that were in charge of her case and for whom the guard wanted to parade the prisoner with her injuries?

While the doctor continued to treat her gums and her hemorrhages, he had to ignore the more serious wounds on her wrists from the handcuffs.

The tight handcuff torture often was used in the prison system of Chairman Mao. A prisoner might have the handcuffs tied to a bar on the window so the prisoner could not eat, drink, or go to the toilet. Sometimes additional chains were put on the ankles. The purpose was to destroy a person's morale. However, since the Communists claimed to have abolished all torture, these treatments were called "punishment" or "persuasion."

After months of exercise, Nien Cheng was able to raise her arms above her head. It was a year before she could stretch them out straight. Because of the nerve damage in her hands, they still ache even today. She has to wear gloves to bed in winter. Her feet were not permanently damaged, but they were painful and swollen for many weeks. Still Nien Cheng tried to brush her hair and zip up her slacks in spite of the pain in doing so. She has remarked, "Looking back on those years, I believe the main reason I was able to survive my ordeal was that the Maoist Revolutionaries failed to break my fighting spirit."[3]

President Nixon poses below the Great Wall of China in February 1972; Nien Cheng felt that United States President Richard Nixon's trip to China in 1972 caused Mao to change his policy and that led to her release.

Chapter 8

RELEASE

During the rest of 1971, Nien Cheng tried to figure out what was happening in the power struggle at the top of the Communist government. There were signs that Lin Biao and the military were losing status and that Zhou Enlai and those favoring international outreach were gaining favor. Since Nien Cheng assumed that her own imprisonment might be due to the military faction's wanting to get evidence against Zhou Enlai, this shift might be favorable to her. The prisoners and the Chinese in general were told of the planned visit of President Richard Nixon of the United States to China in February 1972.

With this hope on the horizon, Nien Cheng planned all the more carefully how she could survive another winter. She desperately needed warm clothing. After five years at the detention house, her jacket and bedding were wearing out. She asked to buy some new things with her money. A week later, a bundle was brought to Nien Cheng's cell. When she opened it, she discovered the winter clothing that the Red Guards in 1966 had permitted her to gather for her daughter, Meiping. Even an unwashed tea mug was included.

Nien Cheng examined the clothing carefully hoping to find

some written message. She found none. She thought that the clothing looked as new as it had in 1966. What had happened to Meiping? Nien Cheng had never received any parcels from her daughter as some of the other prisoners had from their families. She thought that perhaps her daughter had been forced to renounce her.

Nien Cheng called the guard to ask about the bundle and what happened to her daughter. The guard responded that nothing had happened, that the daughter probably bought new clothes. Nien Cheng wanted to believe that her daughter was still alive, but the evidence of the clothes disproved that. Her emotional turmoil and anxiety coupled with her poor physical condition resulted in a high fever and delirium. She was sent back to the prison hospital for a short time.

The discovery of her daughter's possessions in that bundle was what Nien Cheng describes as "the worst moment."[1] Prayer helped her, but she could not pray openly in prison. Often she would pray while pretending to read Mao's books.

Her faith was very important to her: "Throughout the years of my imprisonment, I had turned to God often and felt His presence. In the drab surroundings of the gray cell, I had known magic moments of transcendence that I had not experienced in the ease and comfort of my normal life. My belief in the ultimate triumph of truth and goodness had been restored, and I had renewed courage to fight on. My faith had sustained me in these the darkest hours of my life and brought me safely through privation, sickness, and torture. At the same time, my suffering had strengthened my faith and made me realize that God was always there. It was up to me to come to Him."[2]

President Nixon's trip to Beijing came in February 1972. In March Nien Cheng was again called for interrogation. This time the interrogator was the original one on her case. He started at the beginning as if nothing had happened in the years he had been away. Nien Cheng thought that perhaps he was serving a different superior than the other ones. He did not seem to be trying to trap her so that he could prove she was lying.

Finally in autumn 1972, the interrogator produced an old letter from the Shell files. It had been written to the new British general manager advising him what to bring to China on his new assignment. The British secretary who had written the letter for Nien Cheng had said that the Shanghai government allowed everyone to buy a certain amount of grain per month that could be used as either rice or flour. Although this was just one item in a long list, the interrogator said that this statement gave the foreigners information about the grain supply. Since all foreigners living in Shanghai already knew this fact, it seemed to Nien Cheng that the interrogator had been instructed to find some reason to justify her imprisonment and not declare her innocent.

That winter, Nien Cheng had another bad hemorrhage. When the bleeding had been brought under control, she finally was taken to the gynecology department of the hospital of the best medical college. The doctor was a young woman with the arm band of the revolutionaries. After a clumsy and brief examination, the doctor said that Nien Cheng had cancer of the uterus. Nien Cheng doubted the diagnosis. She thought the woman was not a qualified doctor. However, her general treatment in the prison improved.

On March 27, 1973, six and a half years after she had been brought to the detention house, Nien Cheng was told to pack up her things and leave. The interrogator read his report to her. It said that she had been brought to the detention house on September 27, 1966, because she had told of the grain supply situation in Shanghai and that she had defended the traitor Liu Shaoqi. However, because she was "politically backward and ignorant" and because she had shown some improvement in her thinking, no charges would be filed against her. She was to be allowed to leave as a free person.

Nien Cheng was furious. She said that she could not accept the conclusion of the report and would stay in the detention house until she was found innocent and an apology for wrongful arrest was made. She denied that she had ever given out any information about the grain supply situation, and she noted that Liu Shaoqi had not yet been denounced when she had been brought to the detention house.

The interrogators were shocked. They had never had a prisoner refuse to leave. They told her that her opinion would be noted and forwarded to the authorities but that she had to leave because the government wanted her to leave. They said that her family was waiting for her outside. Then two guards dragged her outside.

Outside at some distance, a young woman waited beside a blue taxi. Was it Meiping? Nien Cheng's heart sank when she realized that the girl was too short. Hean, her goddaughter, had come to meet her.

Hean guided her to the taxi. Nien Cheng asked for Meiping. Hean did not reply but squeezed her hand. The two rode in silence to her new home. The government had allocated two rooms upstairs in a shabby house to Nien Cheng. The standard furniture usually given to newly married couples and a servant were included, because it was assumed that she could not care for herself.

When they arrived at the new place, Hean hugged Nien Cheng and told her how good it was to have her back. Hean explained that her mother was going to come, but at the last minute was called to go to a meeting. Hean's silence about Meiping told Nien Cheng the news she did not want to hear. Hean introduced A-yi, the new servant. In private Hean warned Nien Cheng to be careful what she said around the servant. Nien Cheng was surprised that servants were still allowed. Hean said that the security bureau had suggested that she find a maid for Nien Cheng because of her illness.

When Nien Cheng was alone with her godchild, she asked

Hean again what had happened to Meiping. Hean told her that her mother had written to Hean to tell her that Meiping had committed suicide. Nien Cheng collapsed in Hean's arms, and they both wept for Meiping. It would have been easier if Nien Cheng had died in prison thinking her daughter was alive. The mother's struggle to win her case to protect her daughter's name seemed meaningless.

Hean said that the security bureau official had told her not to say anything about Meiping. Someone from the revolutionary committee of the film studio would notify Nien Cheng tomorrow. However, Hean wondered if they would ever know what really happened to Meiping. No one would dare talk about her death.

Nien Cheng vowed to herself that she would find out what happened to Meiping. She would have to be very careful and not let anyone—even Hean—know that she intended to do so because then the authorities would try to stop her.

So Nien Cheng asked Hean about herself and learned that her godchild had been married and had two children. Hean did not live in Shanghai. She had been called there by the security bureau to help Nien Cheng get settled. But she would have to leave in a few weeks.

Before Hean left, she was able to help Nien Cheng get dental attention. Nien Cheng was to have her teeth pulled because of the gum infection. Later that day, Nien Cheng looked at herself in a mirror for the first time in six and a half years, she was shocked to see the changes in her face—now colorless and with sunken cheeks. She weighed only 85 pounds—down from her normal 115.

The next day the delegation from the film studio visited Nien Cheng. She asked them about the circumstances of her daughter's death. The two men from the film studio replied that Meiping had jumped out the ninth floor window of the Shanghai Athletics Association building in the early morning of June 16, 1967. She had been taken there for questioning by the Revolutionaries. Why she was being questioned was unimportant, because committing suicide was considered a crime against socialism. To Nien Cheng's inquiry about investigations of the death or a coroner's report, the men replied that they did not know because it was a time of unrest when there were many suicides. Nien Cheng was told how she could secure the ashes of her daughter from the crematorium. She told the men that she would make a formal request to have her daughter's death investigated.

The two men left some diaries that had belonged to Meiping and a sum of money that was normally paid to the family of a deceased worker. As they left her, one of the men said: "From what we heard at the film studio, your daughter was well thought of by her colleagues and fellow workers. We regret that because of her unfortunate family background she could not assume a correct attitude towards the Great Proletarian Cultural Revolution."[3]

Nien Cheng wrote a letter to some of her daughter's friends at the film studio and asked them to visit her. When the friends came, they could not add much to the account of Meiping's death. They did doubt that Meiping had committed suicide, because she was not the type to do so. They also questioned what she was doing at the Athletics Association building. The Revolutionaries from the film studio would have interrogated her at the studio. The other building had been taken over by an organization attached to the militia. They had heard that a secret court had been set up there. They cautioned Nien Cheng that because of the uncertain political situation, not much could be done then to investigate Meiping's death.

With money from her bank accounts returned to her, Nien Cheng had enough to reward people who helped her. Through Hean's mother, she was able to see a gynecologist. She did not have cancer. She was diagnosed as having acute hormone disturbance, probably caused by anxiety and stress. After a hysterectomy Nien Cheng spent three weeks recovering in a hospital ward and then went home. After all her teeth had been extracted, she was fitted for dentures.

Nien Cheng set about organizing her new life. She gave private lessons in English to students who wanted to learn. She knew that she had to be very careful because her servant, her neighbors, her students, and even some of her old friends were required to spy on her and report to others about her. However, her kindness to even these spies won some of them over to give her assistance and information—though of course they still had to go on spying for others. With her daughter dead, the thought of leaving China occurred to Nien Cheng, although this dream seemed impossible to accomplish.

Nien Cheng was determined to find the facts of her daughter's death, but she had to be careful. She decided to go secretly to look at the building, the Athletics Association, from which her daughter was supposed to have jumped. She even talked with some of the people who lived in the neighborhood. Nien Cheng saw that the barred windows were so narrow that there was a question of whether someone could have jumped from them. Even more significant, she learned that in 1967 there had been scaffolding around the building—making a jump even more unlikely.

On one of her walks, Nien Cheng bumped into her old gardener who was delighted to see her. Nien Cheng told him that she wanted to give him the gratuity that she had planned years ago, but he said that Meiping had given him the money. Nien Cheng knew it must have taken almost all the money in Meiping's savings to do so and she was proud that her daughter had done so. The gardener put Nien Cheng in touch with two of her other servants. One of them had kept in contact with Meiping and had made inquiries after her death. He had been told that Meiping had been taken by a group of revolutionaries in the middle of the night.

As more of Meiping's friends learned of Nien Cheng's release from prison, they visited her. Sun Kai, the young man Meiping was planning to marry once her mother was released, told Nien Cheng that he had gone to the film studio and the crematorium when he learned of Meiping's death that day. He did not think Meiping committed suicide. He had learned that the men who forced Meiping to go with them were acting on orders from leaders in Shanghai who had some relationship to the investigation of Nien Cheng's case. Sun Kai warned Nien Cheng that her life might be in danger if the officials responsible for Meiping's death thought that the mother did not believe the story of the suicide.

Not long after, Mr. Hu, the friend of her husband who had visited her before she was taken to the detention house, paid a visit to Nien Cheng. Mr. Hu's wife and mother had died of heart attacks during the Cultural Revolution because the hospitals had refused to treat the family of a capitalist. Nien Cheng thanked Mr. Hu for the advice about not giving false confessions that he had given her back in 1966. (Later on, Mr. Hu asked Nien Cheng to marry him, but she declined with the face-saving explanation that she had promised her late husband always to remain Mrs. Cheng.)

Mr. Hu did tell Nien Cheng that her case was often mentioned in connection with Meiping's death. His party secretary had told him that Nien Cheng's arrest was because of the investigation of a conspiracy of foreign companies and government departments. The party secretary had implied that either Lin Biao or Jiang Qing (the wife of Mao Zedong) wanted to use confessions of people like Nien Cheng against Premier Zhou Enlai.

Even though Premier Zhou Enlai seemed to be in power, Nien Cheng was aware that the political power struggle at the top levels of the Communist party was still being fought. She knew that there were people spying on her and even setting traps for her. Sometimes the traps were baited with ideas of how she could get back at Meiping's murderer. Someone also was trying to make life in her neighborhood uncomfortable for her by writing signs that she was a spy and getting children to taunt her. Once someone on a bicycle ran into her, pushing her in front of a bus that stopped just in time to prevent killing her.

When she told one of her students whom she knew to be a spy and in the militia about this incident, he advised her to be more meek and resigned. He warned her that she had powerful enemies but also people who felt sorry for her. The political struggle at top government levels had reached a critical stage.

The top leadership in China was undergoing changes. First Premier Zhou Enlai died. His death meant the end of the conspiracy theory that had caused Nien Cheng's arrest. Chairman Mao Zedong was terminally ill at the time. On one side was Jiang Qing and her three companions, called "the Gang of Four"; on the other side was the more moderate faction with Deng Xiaoping. The Jiang Qing group became alarmed at the numbers of people who came to Tiananmen Square in Beijing to pay tribute to Zhou Enlai. They ordered the police and the militia to drive the people away. Thousands of mourners were killed. It was said that it took two days to wash away the blood and remove everything, including corpses, from the square.

In September 1976, Mao Zedong died. By October, Jiang Qing and the others of the Gang of Four were arrested. The more moderate faction had won. Nien Cheng planned to submit petitions asking that she be declared rehabilitated—not just released because of illness or reeducation. She also wanted her daughter's death investigated. She had learned that the men that had taken her daughter had not been ordered to kill her. Instead, they overdid the torture intended to get Meiping to denounce her mother.

Chapter 9

REHABILITATION

Nien Cheng wrote many petitions for rehabilitation and investigations, but none were answered until 1978, when an official from the public security bureau visited her. He told her that her case would be reviewed, but first the government had to review the many cases of people still in prison. Then they would review situations of people like herself who were on the outside, and finally the cases of those who had died, like her daughter.

At last, in October 1978, representatives of the public security bureau called on Nien Cheng to apologize for her wrongful arrest and imprisonment. They offered condolences on the death of her daughter as a result of persecution. They asked for her approval of the wording of her rehabilitation document that found her not guilty of any crime. Nien Cheng responded that she felt no resentment, but that she wanted her daughter's murderer brought to justice.

The Shanghai Film Studio held a memorial for Meiping that was attended by more than two hundred of her friends and colleagues. It was a simple and dignified service. The memorial speech given by Meiping's teacher emphasized her student's many accomplishments during her twenty-four years of life. Afterward, people came forward to bow to Meiping's photograph and shake hands with Nien Cheng.

Newspaper accounts of Meiping's memorial service and Nien Cheng's rehabilitation brought many visitors. Relatives that had kept their distance while Nien Cheng was under suspicion returned with offers of help. They did not think they needed to explain their earlier neglect because they had behaved as so many others had under Mao Zedong's rule. With the money from the bank accounts released to her, Nien Cheng made gifts to relatives of her husband and herself, to the young people who had helped her, to her old servants, and to widows of former Shell staff members. She also contributed sixty thousand yuan (forty thousand dollars in 1978) for a program to rebuild nursery schools and day-care centers destroyed by the Red Guards.

With the establishment of diplomatic relations between China and the United States, Nien Cheng seriously considered a plan to leave China. She wanted to get a passport while the political climate was favorable. One day, on the "Voice of America" radio news program, she heard that China was seeking most-favored-nation status with the United States for trade purposes. She recalled that one of the requirements for this status was that countries could not block family reunions. This rule had been adopted by the United States originally to help Jews in the Soviet Union get to Israel.

Nien Cheng immediately wrote to one of her sisters in the

United States asking to be sent an invitation to visit her for a "family reunion." Her sister responded immediately with a suitable letter. Next Nien Cheng secured an application for a passport—a step in the bureaucratic system that was not guaranteed. After she had submitted her application, she knew it might be at least a year before she would hear about it.

It was 1979 when she received an official letter from the bureau responsible for sorting looted goods. Nien Cheng did not think that she would recover anything of value, but when she went to the bureau, she was told that some of her porcelain pieces had been located. The Shanghai Museum was interested in purchasing fifteen of the pieces. Her efforts to save some of her porcelain when the Red Guards looted her house had not been wasted. At least some of the antique pieces had survived.

Nien Cheng was not enthusiastic about giving the items to a government institution such as the museum. However, she knew that she could not take her collection with her if she left the country. She decided to donate the porcelain. As a reward, she was given a special ceremony and presented with a certificate of merit. She was given a reproduction of an ancient scroll that she was able to take with her to the United States.

Still Nien Cheng tried to pursue the matter of bringing Meiping's murderer to justice. One of the problems was that the Cultural Revolution had not then been officially repudiated. Many of the revolutionaries who had committed crimes then had since joined the party. It was more difficult to accuse such a person of a crime.

One day a neighbor told her that the man who was responsible for Meiping's death had been taken into custody. He was being questioned about a number of other deaths as well. Since Nien Cheng could not confirm the rumor and since she was given no official notice, she discounted the report. However, a week after she had left Shanghai in 1981, she read in a Hong Kong newspaper that a man had been publicly tried for the death of Meiping and five other victims. The families of the other five attended the trial. The man was sentenced to death but given a suspended sentence of two years.

Nien Cheng realized that the security bureau had waited for her to leave the country before scheduling the trial because the family of victims were always invited to express their agreement with the verdict and sentence. The government knew from her petitions that she would have objected to the suspended sentence. Meiping's murderer went free in China after serving only two years.

Nien Cheng thought the Chinese New Year of February 1980 would be the last she would celebrate in China. She decided to have a big celebration for her students and young friends who had helped her so much since she left the detention house. She had "foreign food" of pork, hamburgers, and tomato soup for over thirty guests. She ordered three large cakes with fresh cream from the bakery. A large assortment of fireworks kept everyone entertained for two hours.

It was not until July that Nien Cheng was given her passport. With some help from a British bank manager, she secured an appointment at the American consulate to obtain her visa. After getting the other foreign visas she needed, she had one last thing she wanted to do. She rented a house near Hangzhou, to go up the mountain for a retreat so she could sort out her feelings about leaving China. She was sad to leave because her attachment to her country is very strong. She knew that once she left, she would not return to China to die.

Nien Cheng left Shanghai on a steamer bound for Hong Kong. A few of her friends accompanied her to the wharf. Under Chinese regulations, she could take only one suitcase and one carry-on bag. She was allowed to take only twenty dollars worth of Hong Kong currency. Her Chinese bank accounts and everything else had to be left behind.

As the ship pulled away, Nien Cheng glimpsed the Shell building and the window of her old office. She felt sad and guilty that it was she and not her daughter that was alive to start a new life. She felt that Meiping's death was the direct result of her decision to return to China in 1949 at her husband's request. She had tried hard to remain true to the country of her birth, but now she was leaving in "a break so final that it was shattering."[1]

Chapter 10

A NEW LIFE

Just as Nien Cheng had to learn to adjust to a different life outside the detention house, now she had to learn about changes in the West. After her stay in Hong Kong, Shell, her former employer, paid for a first-class ticket on the jet that carried her across the Pacific Ocean.

Nien Cheng spent a year visiting friends and relatives and looking for a place to live. Canada offered her a home, and she spent two years in Ottawa. The winter weather and winds there were hard for her because of her sensitivity to the cold from her torture. In 1983, she moved to Washington, D.C., as a legal immigrant sponsored by her sister. She purchased a one-bedroom condominium and learned the ways of the freeways, supermarkets, and automated bank tellers.

Nien Cheng worked on her book, *Life and Death in Shanghai*, which was first published in 1986 and later issued in paperback in 1988. Some of her story was printed in *Time* magazine as part of the cover feature. Her book was praised by the critics as both extraordinarily well-written and a remarkable account of life in China during the Cultural Revolution. Not only did Nien Cheng give an account of what happened to her, but she also portrayed the effect of that revolution on the lives of many other people.

Her new life in the United States has been a busy one. She has come to feel at home in a nation of immigrants and persons fleeing persecution. She loves the freedom to speak without having to worry whether her words are politically correct. Here the police and the political parties perform different functions than they did in China, where they spied on the lives of the Chinese. She enjoys the wealth of information available to her through books, magazines, and newspapers.

Nien Cheng still keeps close watch on the conditions in China. She was glad when the Cultural Revolution was declared a national catastrophe, but she is sorry that the Communist party in China has been unwilling to overthrow the policies of Mao Zedong. She writes: "Constant change is an integral part of the Communist philosophy. For the entire thirty-eight years of Communist rule in China, the Party's policy has swung like a pendulum from left to right and back again without stop. Unless and until a political system rooted in law, rather than personal power, is firmly established in China, the road to the future will always be full of twists and turns."[1]

Nien Cheng's prediction has been accurate. When the Chinese students flocked into Tiananmen Square in 1989 to call for greater democracy, many were killed by the Chinese army. When Nien Cheng saw these scenes on television, she started to cry, remembering Meiping's death and thinking of the parents of the slaughtered students. During this crisis, the television programs in the United States often featured her expert analysis of the situation. She was broadcast in both Chinese and English on the "Voice of America" radio network that could be heard in China. She often talks with Chinese who are studying in the United States.

Of the 1989 uprising, she has said: "The massacre of the pro-democracy demonstrators in Peking is but a painful episode in the Chinese people's struggle for democratic change that started more than seventy years ago."[2] She believes that much of the traditional culture will have to be changed.

In 1988, Nien Cheng became an American citizen. She does not want to return to China, because of the memories of Meiping's death. Instead she has found a way of helping American students and honoring Meiping by establishing an annual scholarship in her daughter's name at the Slippery Rock University in Pennsylvania, where most of the students are from working-class backgrounds. She reports: "America has given me a new home. I like to show my gratitude in a concrete way. This is now my country."[3]

Although readers of her book discover in Nien Cheng a woman of extraordinary courage and fortitude, she, herself, denies that she is a hero. "I did what I believed right. That was all. There comes a time in life one has to make a major decision. It just happened that I was lucky President Nixon came to China and that caused Mao to change his policy. I was released. Otherwise, I would have died in prison. I would like my readers to think I was just like anybody else in China whose fate was unfortunately in the hands of a cruel regime which cared more for power than the suffering of its people."4

NOTES

Chapter 1

1. Nien Cheng, *Life and Death in Shanghai* (New York: Grove Press, 1986; London: Grafton Books, HarperCollins Publishers Limited, 1986; New York: Viking Penguin, 1988), 70.
2. Ibid.
3. Ibid., 71.
4. Ibid.
5. Ibid.
6. Ibid.
7. Ibid., 74.
8. Ibid., 80.
9. Ibid., 95.

Chapter 2

1. Cheng, *Life and Death in Shanghai*, 88.

Chapter 3

1. Cheng, *Life and Death in Shanghai*, 120.
2. Ibid., 122.
3. Ibid., 131.
4. Ibid., 141.

Chapter 4

1. Cheng, *Life and Death in Shanghai*, 144.
2. Ibid., 155.
3. Ibid., 171.

Chapter 6

1. Cheng, *Life and Death in Shanghai*, 226.
2. Ibid., 240.
3. Ibid., 245.
4. Ibid., 256.

Chapter 7

1. Cheng, *Life and Death in Shanghai*, 299.
2. Ibid., 308.
3. Ibid., 329.

Chapter 8

1. E. Vaughn, "The Resolve to Resist," *Christianity Today* (May 13, 1988), 21.
2. Cheng, *Life and Death in Shanghai*, 346-47.
3. Ibid., 369.

Chapter 9

1. Cheng, *Life and Death in Shanghai*, 535.

Chapter 10

1. Cheng, *Life and Death in Shanghai*, 543.

2. Nien Cheng, "Massacre in Peking," *National Review* (August 4, 1989), 31.

3. C. Reeve, "A Voice of Hope for China," *New Choices for the Best Years*, (September 1989), 10.

4. N. Cheng, Letter dated February 23, 1991.

Nien Cheng (1915 -)

1915 Nien Cheng is born in Beijing. Japan invades German-controlled Chinese territory of Kiaochow, Shandong Province. Germans sink the British passenger ship *Lusitania* and U.S. merchant ships and blockade Britain with submarines. Telegraph service is opened between Japan and the United States.

1916 Woodrow Wilson is reelected U.S. president.

1917 Czar Nicholas III of Russia is overthrown and the Bolsheviks seize power. U.S. declares war on Germany and enters World War I.

1918 World War I ends. Daylight saving time begins in U.S.

1919 Versailles Conference awards Kiaochow to Japan; China refuses to sign the Treaty of Paris. U.S. passes Eighteenth Amendment, prohibiting the sale of alcoholic beverages. First League of Nations meeting is held in Paris.

1920 The Panama Canal opens. U.S. passes Nineteenth Amendment giving women the right to vote. The League of Nations is established.

1921 First Congress of the Chinese Communist party (CCP) is held. Albert Einstein wins Nobel Prize in physics.

1922 The Union of Soviet Socialist Republics (U.S.S.R.) is established. Benito Mussolini becomes dictator of Italy.

1923 The left and the right wings of Kuomintang (KMT)—the Chinese Nationalist party—are created. Mustafa Kamal Pasha (Ataturk) establishes the Republic of Turkey. Nazi party leader Adolf Hitler is imprisoned for an unsuccessful coup attempt.

1924 U.S. severely restricts immigration.

1925 Hitler organizes the Nazi party and publishes volume one of *Mein Kampf.*

1926 Germany is admitted to the League of Nations.

1927 Charles A. Lindbergh makes the first solo airplane flight.

1928 The Nationalists, under Chiang Kai-shek, unite China under one government; the National government moves to Nanjing. Walt Disney releases the first Mickey Mouse film.

1929 U.S. stock market crashes; Great Depression begins; worldwide economic crisis follows.

1930 Hitler's Nazi party gains a majority in German elections.

1931 Japan invades and occupies Manchuria, Mongolia, and China.

1932 Franklin D. Roosevelt wins landslide presidential victory.

1933 U.S. passes Twenty-first Amendment repealing Prohibition.

1934 The CCP, led by Mao Zedong, begins the 500-mile-long march to Shensi Province.

1935 Mass student demonstrations in China lead to the creation of an anti-Japanese leftist movement. Nien Cheng goes to Great Britain for further studies.

1936 Chiang Kai-shek is kidnapped by KMT. Franklin D. Roosevelt is reelected president. Mussolini and Hitler proclaim the Rome-Berlin Axis.

1937 Nanjing falls to the Japanese.

1939 Francisco Franco becomes dictator of Spain. Germany invades Poland; World War II begins (ends 1945).

1940 Nien Cheng, with her husband, moves back to China from London. Roosevelt is elected president for a third time.

103

1941 The Chengs live in the city of Chongqing, which is bombarded by Japanese. Germany invades the Soviet Union. Japanese bomb Pearl Harbor; U.S. and Great Britain declare war on Japan.

1942 Nien Cheng's daughter, Meiping, is born in Sydney, Australia.

1945 U.S. drops first atomic bombs on Hiroshima and Nagasaki, Japan; Hitler commits suicide; Mussolini is killed; Germany and Japan surrender to Allies; World War II ends. China regains control of Manchuria and Taiwan. The United Nations is established.

1946 United States grants independence to the Philippines. Winston Churchill of Great Britain gives "Iron Curtain" speech. United Nations General Assembly holds its first session in London.

1947 India and Pakistan become independent nations. U.S. Secretary of State George Marshall proposes the European Recovery Program, also called the Marshall Plan.

1949 The Chinese Communist party (CCP) conquers China. People's Republic of China (PRC) is proclaimed, with CCP chairman Mao Zedong as its leader. Nien Cheng and Meiping visit Hong Kong. Possession of firearms becomes illegal in China. Eleven Communists in the U.S. are convicted of conspiracy to overthrow the government.

1950 Kang-chi Cheng becomes general manager of Shell International Petroleum Company in Shanghai. Nien Cheng has one of her kidneys removed. A thirty-year Sino-Soviet treaty is signed. Korean War begins (ends 1953). U.S. agrees to send arms and troops to Taiwan and Vietnam.

1951 U.S. Congress passes Twenty-second Amendment, setting two terms (eight years) as the maximum service for president. Color television is introduced in the U.S.

1952 Richard M. Nixon is elected vice-president of the United States. King George VI of England dies; his daughter, Elizabeth II, becomes queen.

1953 Korean armistice ends war. Korea is divided along 38th parallel into North Korea and South Korea. China institutes its first five-year plan to promote industrialization. Joseph Stalin of the U.S.S.R. dies. Nikita Khrushchev becomes head of Soviet Communist Party Central Committee.

1954 Communists in Vietnam take Dien Bien Phu and occupy Hanoi. Vietnam becomes divided.

1955 China begins a big push for agricultural collectivization by organizing farmers into agriculture producers' cooperatives. U.S. begins sending aid to Vietnam. Dictator Juan Perón of Argentina is overthrown.

1956 Hungarians revolt against Soviet occupation of their country; Soviet troops invade Hungary. Israeli army invades Sinai Peninsula. Pakistan declares itself an Islamic country. Gamal Abdul Nasser becomes president of Egypt.

1957 In a so-called anti-rightist campaign, many Chinese dissidents are sent for reeducation in labor camps. Kang-chi Cheng dies of cancer; Nien Cheng starts working as an adviser to the management of Shell. Nien Cheng's brother is interrogated several times and is removed from his post by the Communists. Andrei Gromyko becomes Soviet foreign minister. Soviets launch first man-made satellites, *Sputnik I* and *Sputnik II*, to circle the earth. European Common Market is established.

1958 China begins the Great Leap Forward (1958-60); government seizes small family plots; emphasis is placed on the development of labor-intensive industries. U.S. launches its first satellite. Alaska becomes forty-ninth state of the U.S. Charles de Gaulle becomes president of France.

1959 Among widespread violence and rebellion against Chinese rule, the Dalai Lama, the Tibetan spiritual leader, takes exile in India. Hawaii becomes fiftieth U.S. state. Liu Shaoqi becomes chairman of the Chinese republic (ousted in 1969). Fidel Castro overthrows Cuban dictator Fulgencio Batista and becomes president.

1960 The Soviet Union terminates its economic aid and pulls all Soviet advisers out of China; Chinese government returns small family plots to people. Richard M. Nixon and John F. Kennedy hold first television debates between presidential candidates; Kennedy defeats Nixon in presidential election. Leonid Brezhnev becomes president of the U.S.S.R.

1961 U.S. breaks diplomatic ties with Cuba. Berlin Wall is erected.

1962 Nien Cheng's mother dies. A serious U.S.-Soviet crisis is avoided when the Soviet Union complies with the American demands to remove missiles from Cuba. U.S. dispatches military advisers to South Vietnam.

1963 President Kennedy is assassinated in Dallas; Lyndon B. Johnson becomes president of the United States. Rev. Martin Luther King, Jr. is arrested in race riots in Birmingham, Alabama.

1964 China becomes the fifth nation in the world to explode a nuclear bomb. Vietnam War escalates. Nikita Khrushchev is ousted in coup; Alexei Kosygin becomes prime minister and Leonid Brezhnev becomes Communist party secretary in U.S.S.R.

1965 U.S.S.R. supplies arms to North Vietnam. Antiwar demonstrations sweep U.S. Great Britain celebrates 750th anniversary of the Magna Carta. Great proletarian Cultural Revolution starts in China (finishes 1969).

1966 The Red Guards, organizations of young people, are formed in China. All Chinese schools and universities are closed to allow students to participate in the Cultural Revolution; more and more students participate in the Red Guard groups. Shell closes its Shanghai office. Nien Cheng's house is invaded by the Red Guards; she is forcibly taken to several "struggle" meetings and sent to a detention house. Zhou Enlai visits Albania and Romania. One million people demonstrate in Tiananmen Square. President Johnson of U.S. tours the Far East.

1967 Red Guards take over the municipal government and invade the British Embassy in Beijing, China. Nien Cheng is interrogated several times in the detention center. Meiping is murdered by Communist revolutionaries. Arab nations and Israel engage in Six-Day War; Israel defeats Arab nations. U.S. bombs Hanoi, North Vietnam. Chinese Embassy personnel are attacked in Moscow. Hydrogen bomb is detonated in China.

1968 Soviet Union invades and occupies Czechoslovakia. Richard Nixon is elected U.S. president. U.S.-North Vietnam Paris Peace talks begin. Soviet Union invades Czechoslovakia. Albania withdraws from Warsaw Pact. Martin Luther King, Jr. is assassinated in Memphis, Tennessee. *Apollo 8* of U.S. is the first spacecraft to orbit the moon.

1969 China declares the Soviet Union its principal enemy. Nien Cheng shares her cell in the detention center with a spy from the Chinese government. Nien Cheng's health deteriorates and she is sent to the hospital several times; interrogations to force her to "confess" her crimes continue. Neil Armstrong of U.S. is the first man to walk on the moon. Ho Chi-Minh, president of the Democratic Republic of Vietnam dies. China carries out first successful underground nuclear test.

1970 After a coup in Cambodia, Prince Norodom Sihanouk establishes a government in exile in Beijing. China launches an earth-orbiting satellite. U.S. invades Cambodia. China establishes diplomatic relations with Canada and Italy.

1971 Henry Kissinger, U.S. national security adviser, makes a secret trip to China. Nien Cheng is abused severely at interrogation meetings; her health deteriorates rapidly; she suspects her daughter Meiping is dead. People's Republic of China is admitted into the United Nations; Taiwan loses its membership. American Ping-Pong team visits China. Chairman Mao invites U.S. president Nixon to China; Lin Biao, head of the Red Army, dies mysteriously in a plane crash in Mongolia.

1972 President Nixon meets with Mao Zedong in Peking. Twenty countries (including Japan and West Germany) establish diplomatic relations with China. China vetoes Bangladesh membership in the UN. Nixon is reelected president; he is the first U.S. president to visit China and Moscow.

1973 U.S. and China exchange liaison offices (diplomatic missions). Nien Cheng is released from the detention center after six-and-a-half years; she finds out for the first time about her daughter's death. Cease-fire is declared in Vietnam. Middle East unrest causes oil prices to double, creating worldwide energy crisis.

1974 Nixon resigns as U.S. president. Arabs lift oil embargo to the West.

1975 Chiang Kai-shek dies and is succeeded by his son, Chiang Ching-Kuo as the KMT chairman. The position of chairman of the republic is abolished in China. Vietnam War ends with South Vietnam's surrender to North Vietnam.

1976 Mao Zedong and Zhou Enlai die in China. In a palace coup soon after Mao's death, Jiang Qing, Mao's widow and the leader of the "Gang of Four," and scores of ranking party and military officials are arrested. Hua Guofeng becomes premier and chairman of the Chinese Communist party. U.S. and U.S.S.R. sign a nuclear arms limitation treaty.

1977 Deng Xiaoping and many ranking officials in China who were purged previously are reinstated.

1978 Deng Xiaoping initiates agricultural reforms in China. Nien Cheng's petition for rehabilitation and investigation is at first delayed by the public security bureau; later the bureau apologizes for her wrongful arrest and imprisonment. A memorial service is held for Meiping. Nien Cheng decides to leave China and move to the West.

1979 Many political prisoners are released from Chinese labor camps. China enforces "One-Couple-One-Child" policy to curb its population growth. U.S. and China establish diplomatic ties. Beijing municipal government bans hanging of pro-democracy posters on Democracy Wall. Margaret Thatcher becomes prime minister of Great Britain. Egypt and Israel sign the Camp David Accords. Islamic fundamentalists, under the leadership of the Ayatollah Ruhollah Khomeini, overthrow the Shah of Iran.

1980 Russian forces invade Afghanistan. Ronald Reagan, a Republican, is elected president of the U.S. Nien Cheng gives private lessons in English.

1981 Nien Cheng leaves China and moves to Canada. Meiping's murderer gets a two-year suspended sentence.

1982 According to the 1982 census, China's population reaches 1 billion. Nixon visits China to commemorate tenth anniversary of reinstatement of U.S.-Chinese relations. Argentina attempts to seize the Falkland Islands, but is defeated by Great Britain.

1983 Chinese government launches a so-called anti-spiritual pollution campaign to restrict foreign (Western) culture and values. Nien Cheng moves to the United States from Canada.

1984 The United Kingdom and China sign an agreement to return Hong Kong to China in 1997. Several industrial reforms are introduced in China.

1985 Mikhail Gorbachev becomes leader of the Soviet Union; he plans to change government through *perestroika* (reconstruction) and *glasnost* (openness).

1986 The Soviet leader Gorbachev calls for better Sino-Soviet relations; Chinese university students march to advocate democracy, human rights, and freedom. Nien Cheng's *Life and Death in Shanghai* is published in New York.

1987 Portugal and China sign an agreement to return the Portuguese colony of Macao to China in 1999. The Dalai Lama gives a speech calling for Tibetan independence before U.S. Congress. Martial law is lifted in Taiwan after 39 years of an authoritarian rule. Pro-independence demonstration takes place in the Tibetan capital city of Lhasa.

1988 Chiang Ching-kuo, president of the Republic of China or Taiwan, dies and is succeeded by Dr. Lee Teng-hui. Sixteen Tibetan monks are killed in pro-independence riots. China relaxes its "One-Couple-One-Child" policy, allowing rural families to have a second child if the first one is a girl. Nien Cheng becomes an American citizen; her book *Life and Death in Shanghai* is published in paperback; she establishes an annual scholarship in her daughter's name at Slippery Rock University in Pennsylvania. George Bush is elected president of the United States.

1989 Communism is rejected by country after country in Eastern Europe. The Berlin Wall is officially opened. Nien Cheng is interviewed on U.S. television for her comments on the pro-democracy unrest in Tiananmen Square in Beijing.

1990 On October 3 East and West Germany are united as the Federal Republic of Germany. Mrs. Thatcher resigns as prime minister of Great Britain and is succeeded by John Major. Nien Cheng visits Hong Kong.

1991 Berlin is designated as the capital of the Federal Republic of Germany. Jiang Qing, widow of Chairman Mao Zedong, commits suicide at the age of 77. Rajiv Gandhi, India's prime minister, is assassinated. Seven Chinese activists, accused of pro-democracy demonstration in 1989, are sentenced in China. Aung San Suu Kyi of Burma (Myanmar) receives the Nobel Peace Prize. Communism fails and the U.S.S.R. faces radical change.

1992 Three members of the Canadian Parliament are expelled from China by Chinese premier Li Peng. Menachem Begin, former prime minister of Israel, dies. Prince Sihanouk returns to Cambodia as head of state.

About the Author

Leila Merrell Foster is a lawyer, United Methodist minister, and clinical psychologist with degrees from Northwestern University and Garrett Evangelical Theological Seminary. She is the author of books and articles on a variety of subjects.

Dr. Foster has traveled in China twice. She felt that Nien Cheng's book, *Life and Death in Shanghai*, helped her understand the situation in China. She admires the courage and faith of Nien Cheng.

Dr. Foster has written other biographies: *Margaret Thatcher—First Woman Prime Minister of Great Britain*, *David Glasgow Farragut—Courageous Navy Commander*, and *The Story of Rachel Carson and the Environmental Movement*.